insight
&
creativity
in Christian
counseling

A study of the usual & the unique

JAY E. ADAMS

TIMELESS TEXTS
WOODRUFF, SC

CONTENTS

Preface   v

Introduction   vii

PART ONE — INSIGHT

1. What Is Insight?   3
2. Selective Insight   5
3. Common Problems and the Counselor's Past   13
4. What to Eliminate   29
5. Bias, Tentativeness, and Insight   34
6. Four Considerations   41

PART TWO — CREATIVITY

7. Who Needs Creativity?   53
8. I Don't Have What It Takes   60
9. Analysis and Synthesis   67
10. Hindrances to Creativity   74
11. The Three Rs   79
12. Review It   94
13. The Old and the New   102
14. Renewal: The Condition for Creativity   112
15. Variety and Adaptation   121

Conclusion   125

Appendix: Insight List   127

Preface
to the Second Printing

I am delighted to see that *Insight and Creativity* is coming back into print under the auspices of TIMELESS TEXTS. The purpose of this book perhaps will be served better in years to come than it has in the past when it had but a scanty distribution. Early on, I began to see budding new counselors falling into wooden patterns of counseling. So I wrote this book to counter that tendency. Now that the movement has spread much more widely there is even greater danger of many more persons canning and refrigerating their counseling approaches.

It is not, of course, that any approach to counseling will do. Every one must be biblical. But within biblical limits, applying the Scriptures to cases of various kinds requires the use of many different ways in which to help people. When Jesus confronted Nicodemus, the woman at the well, and the man born blind, He dealt with each differently, although His message was the same. He baldly said to Nicodemus, "You must be born again." To the woman He talked of water and wells and husbands before presenting the good news. And it was only after the man born blind was healed that He discussed his spiritual condition with him. In each case, Jesus "knew what was in man," and adapted His approach accordingly. The biblical counselor must learn to do so too.

It is my hope, then, that this book will find wide acceptance, because it fills a space that for too long has remained empty. It contains a challenge that every biblical counselor must face and shows him how to meet it successfully. My prayer is that it may help many counselors to help many people.

INTRODUCTION

The two important factors in counseling with which this book is concerned are often thought (wrongly) to be inborn qualities or special gifts that, accordingly, one either has or doesn't have. People (even Christian people) may be heard to say such things as, ''Oh, I just don't have a creative bone in my body,'' or ''Don't expect me to show any insight into what others think; I can't do it. That's just the way I am and the way I'll always be.'' I challenge both claims.

For years I have taught both preaching and counseling, two skills that require insight and creativity for success. And regularly I have seen persons, who at the outset had little insight and no creativity to speak of, develop it to a high degree under proper guidance and direction.

Certainly, there is no question in my mind that anyone with the basic pastoral gifts, and other Christians as well, can learn both. Some will learn more than others, to be sure; yet I am convinced that any faithful student of the Scriptures, rightly guided and motivated, can make great improvements in his skills in both areas. But he must begin by believing that he can make these changes; otherwise, he will get nowhere.

You may wonder how I dare affirm that all and sundry who are Christians can learn the basic skills of insight and creativity. ''Aren't you promising more than you can deliver?'' you may ask. The reason I am sure about this assertion is that I know the Bible requires every Christian to counsel. I have shown this in *Competent to Counsel* and in *Ready to Restore,* a book on counseling for laymen. It is also true because, in order to counsel well, one must acquire biblical insight and must become a creative person. In this book, therefore, it is my purpose to teach you what insight and creativity are and to explain to you some of the ways and the means you may use to develop these two capabilities so important for effective biblical counseling.

Certainly the basic gifts for teaching, exhortation and preaching involve heightened capabilities for obtaining insight and developing creativity, but it is still true that those who do not possess these capabilities in such profusion, through the proper sort of instruction, disciplined practice and prayerful concern, nevertheless, may learn much about their acquisition, development, and use. There are, in the average Christian, native endowments sufficient to handle all the counseling situations in which God calls him or her to minister. But these endowments do not function automatically, any more than other native capabilities do. Like all others, these abilities must be recognized, considered, studied, and developed under the power of the Spirit in accordance with the principles of His Word.

But why should we be concerned about insight and creativity? Precisely because it is the lack of these qualities that so often leads to failure in counseling. And if we are really concerned about our calling to help others (cf. Gal. 6:1, 2; Col. 3:16, etc.), we must not neglect any effort that may make us more able to do so. Some excuse or explain failure in counseling in other ways (and, of course, there are many mistakes that one may make in counseling), but when each failure is examined carefully, in addition to other factors, the marks of poor insight and/or uncreative counseling also are almost always evident. Some of these marks consist of the tendency to focus on the trivial or the peripheral, the overuse of routine, the standardization of approach, a stereotyping of persons and situations, a confounding of primary and secondary (or complicating) problems, the failure to distinguish things that differ, confusion of ordinary and extraordinary factors, and an inflexibility in both the selection and use of Scripture. All the correct doctrine, all the good intentions, that one may muster, will not assist the counselor if he does not have insight into the lives of the persons whom he counsels. All the insight will not do the job if the counselor does not know how to relate the biblical truths to the situation at hand in such a way that the two fit appropriately.

Insight into the inner workings of sinful human beings, into their outer circumstances and problems, and into the correct meaning and applicability of appropriate Bible passages is absolutely essential to counseling. Until a counselor understands what is happening to an individual and what is going on in his particular case, counseling will falter.

Likewise, the importance of creativity in approach, in relationships, in the use of methods and techniques and (above all) in the implementation of biblical principles in the lives of counselees cannot be minimized. It is creativity that particularizes the common, fitting together the usual and the unusual in each situation. Without it, people are crammed into molds they don't fit; rather, the truth must be adapted and applied (but not accommodated) to each person as he is.

Though in some respects opposites, in other ways insight and creativity are similar. In one respect, creativity may be considered more closely related to form, and insight to substance. Working together, they very clearly demonstrate how form affects substance. But the form/substance distinction, though useful for purposes of analysis, is not absolute. The bifurcation of life that this formulation suggests is artificial, not actual. For instance, in the language of counseling, as in the sacraments, because mode *conveys* meaning, change of mode *affects* meaning. If you call a counselee's sin problem "sickness," you will point him to the physician rather than to Jesus Christ as the solution to his problem.[1]

Many who wish to counsel biblically, much like many who wish to preach biblically, erroneously focus all their attention and their energies on substance ("content is the thing") to the neglect of form. But what they do not recognize is that in doing so, they allow the precious biblical substance that they have taken such pains to extract, to be molded, manipulated, distorted, and misused by the ill-fitting form in which they present it. The most perfectly shaped body looks ludicrous in clothes five sizes too small or three sizes too large. As a result of this lack of concern about form, counselors communicate to the counselee something other than they want to communicate; and often their failure closes down significant communication altogether. This, as I said, can be as true in counseling as it is in preaching. Since the two are but two sides of one ministry of the Word (one private, one public), most of what pertains to the one pertains also to the other. Insight and creativity, therefore, can be neglected by the Christian counselor only at peril to his counselee. Without both of them a counselor becomes a Job's comforter, leaving the counselee with all sorts of pious advice that does not fit his case, while doing nothing to really help him lift his burden.

---

1. On this matter in depth, see my book, *The Language of Counseling.*

Moreover, insight and creativity work together. They are, in some respects, two sides of the same door. Insight into the lives of counselees, into their problems (and the settings of each), and into the biblical passages that pertain to what one finds, leads to data that demand and point to the need for creative confrontation of counselees and adaptation of biblical principles to their problems. And it is clear insight into these data that indicates the sort of creativity that is needed. There can hardly be a successful use of the one without the other. Insight is needed to uncover the facts, creativity to deal with them. Insight, therefore, issues the call to creativity; creativity, on the other hand, comes to grips with the unusual, with which insight dare not meddle, by enriching the ordinary and the routine through the process of adaptation.

But neither true biblical insight nor creativity may attempt to do the job on its own. Each, in its own way, contributes; the one provides the flexibility that is necessary to adjust to each particular case, while the other produces the framework and the base for what is to be adapted. The one is varied and may take any number of routes, the other is absolute and fixed. One works with God's own way of describing human activity and responding to it, while the other is a manifestation of the numerous legitimate possibilities for adaptation of those responses that exist within the biblical framework and that grow out of and are appropriate to the biblical base. One deals with principle and the other with practice. Neither, when rightly employed, doing what it was intended to do, has ever led a revolt against the other. They were intended to be comrades, working side by side in the cause of Christian counseling. Insight does not hold reins on creativity in such a way that it is hampered in doing its duty, and creativity never breaks out of the bounds of biblical principle. As the psalmist put it, "Your commandment is very broad" (Ps. 119:96).[2]

For these, and for other reasons that will become apparent as we proceed, we shall devote ourselves to a study of these two important subjects not just academically but in an endeavor to help you to improve your powers of insight and creativity, so that you may be able to serve Jesus Christ as a Christian counselor more faithfully than ever before.

---

2. The Hebrew word translated "broad" means "spacious, wide, expansive" and speaks of the ability of biblical precepts to anticipate and cover all life situations. It speaks also of their inherent power to adapt to the peculiar contours of each. The two words *very* and *broad* double the intensity of the thought in order to emphasize the point.

PART ONE

INSIGHT

1

WHAT IS INSIGHT?

Neither the term *insight* nor the term *creativity* is a prominent biblical word, though unmistakably the concepts they convey may be found throughout the Scriptures. In some modern versions of the Bible the word *insight* appears in both the Old and the New Testaments.[1] The basic idea behind the English word *insight* is clear: to have insight means to be able to *look* deeply enough *into* some matter, *into* some situation or *into* someone's life to apprehend the true nature of what is observed. Usually it refers to the ability to penetrate more deeply into the object, situation, or life than those who, because they lack this skill, are able to see only what lies on or near the surface. A person with insight is capable of discerning *underlying* factors, *inner* characteristics and *hidden* causes and relationships.[2]

As I use the word insight, it is a richer, fuller term than understanding, which may or may not refer to something at a level of depth. Insight includes understanding, but it is an understanding that reaches to everything essential in a situation and penetrates to every depth.[3] Understanding may be partial or incorrect; in contrast, the word *insight* refers to what is always true and complete.

But insight refers not only to correct understanding; it is also closely associated with a wisdom that is coupled to a knowledge of facts that (1) enables one to see individual facts in relationship to wholes, and (2) enables one to see errors, needs, inconsistencies, etc., that demand some sort of change. To me, in short, *insight* is simply the modern English term that brings together the totality of positive meanings found in the three biblical words *knowledge, wisdom,* and *understanding.*

1. Cf. Prov. 1:2 (NIV); 1:4 (Berkeley); Eph. 1:18; Phil. 1:9; Col. 1:9 (NEB).

2. Sometimes the word is used of intuitive flashes of comprehension; in this book, I do not include that meaning. If I had the space I would argue that these "flashes" have an unperceived background that corresponds to the process of insight that I shall describe.

3. *Proper* knowledge and interpretation of the facts is what I mean by the understanding that is involved in insight.

A counselor needs insight in counseling at several points. Sometimes these stand in relationship to each other as steps in a process, but more often they are bound up with one another much as a melody is repeated and retraced over against itself in a round (e.g., "Row, row, row your boat").

First, there must be some knowledge and understanding of what the counselee's problem is and what he has been doing about it. But in the counselor's search for more data, even as he begins to sing "gently down the stream," another side of the counselor's mind takes up the refrain and also begins to sing "Row, row, row your boat" at the same time but from the viewpoint of interpretation (What do these data mean? How are they to be classified, labeled and understood biblically?). As the round progresses, tentative conclusions are reached, modified and rejected. Then, as the first two voices continue singing "merrily, merrily, merrily, merrily" and "gently down the stream," a third may be heard joining in ("Row, row, row your boat"). It is the voice of biblical problem solving saying, "Well, if such-and-such is true, and it means so-and-so according to the Scriptures, then God says that this-and-that must be done about it. Once more, the mind is tentatively putting together ways of possibly meeting situations as they come into clearer and clearer focus. Knowledge and understanding of the problem of related Scriptures, wedded with wisdom that brings these together in a workable way that is within the biblical framework, therefore, is what constitutes counseling insight.

What we see in this mental round, in which several strains of thought interplay and interlace in roughly logical order, is a sketch of the process of insight at work. My statement of the actual happening is, of course, greatly simplified for our purposes but, nevertheless, gives some indication of what, in fact, goes on as an effective counselor listens to, weighs, and works with the data that he is gathering during the counseling process. After all else is boiled away, what remains is the interfacing of data about the counselee with data from the Scriptures. So, we may say that insight is the ability to see the counseling situation as the Scriptures describe it.

In this process, the first thing necessary is the need for selectivity. It is about that all-important point that we shall think in the next chapter.

2

SELECTIVE INSIGHT

One of the prime skills that any counselor with insight has developed is the ability to pare away all that is irrelevant, inconsequential, and otherwise unimportant to an analysis of the counselee's problem. He goes for the jugular! His concern is to pinpoint, surgically, what is crucial while laying aside all else. And what he looks for in the mass of data gathered is the usual, the ordinary; he looks for evidence of something present that is expected, that he already understands.

Jesus demonstrated an amazing ability to do just this. With Nicodemus, with the woman at the well, with the rich young ruler, He penetrated deeply through layers of other material, going directly to the heart of each person's problem.

The Pharisee came as a representative of his group (*"We* know that you are a teacher. . . ."). But he also knew that his own life was lacking in the one thing necessary for meaning and for happiness.[1] Jesus answered the official question (note the plural "we" and "you"), but He also became very personal, sensing Nicodemus' inner desire (note the singular "you").[2] That was insight. Jesus knew Nicodemus' problem. It was the common problem of every Pharisee. He had a "form of godliness" but lacked "the power thereof."

The rich young ruler comes thinking that he is good, that he has kept God's commandments adequately. But his standard of goodness also is outward conformity to the law. Jesus *sees* this. And, with a command growing out of the insight He exposes the young man's inner worship of money: "Go sell. . . ." What others could not see—the common hypocrisy, selfishness, and idolatry of man—was perfectly clear to the Lord Jesus. It was expected, understood. The facts that he was rich,

---

1. Perhaps he volunteered to come for this very reason.

2. All through this exchange, the plurals and the singulars are of significance, sometimes referring to Jesus ("I") and to John the Baptist ("we"), to Nicodemus ("you," sing.), and to the Pharisees that he represented ("you," plur.).

young, a respected ruler, and that he lived an outwardly exemplary lifestyle were all laid aside as Jesus penetrated through them to the *ordinary* underlying problem: sinful selfishness. Others saw the *unusual* externals; Jesus saw the *common* problem of sin.

The woman at the well wanted to argue theology, but she needed forgiveness. Jesus by-passed the former with a quick, authoritative response and instead put his finger on the sore spot: "Call your husband." All sorts of possible distractions, on which many counselors would have allowed themselves to become sidetracked, are nimbly sidestepped as He does so. Again, the *unusual* is eliminated and the *ordinary,* the expected, becomes a matter of focus. Because sin is common to all men (with the exception of Jesus alone), in counseling it is always wise, as Henry Brandt has often said, to look for the sin.

In all three of these accounts, we see Christ's *insight* into the person's problem and into what God wants him to do about it. Coupled with creative adaptation, to which I shall come later on in the book, these instances provide precisely the sort of help that we need in order to learn not only what insight is, but how to develop it.

In this chapter, as I have said, we are concerned to learn something about the importance of *selectivity of data* as it pertains to insight. In each case we have seen Jesus *eliminating* many of the more prominent features as he zeroes in on the truly significant matter. The three accounts were not designed primarily to teach the process of insight (though they do make a point about its existence: cf. John 2:25, Jesus "knew what was in human beings"); they do not tell us much about how Jesus was able to gather and interpret the data and make His judgments. But they do exhibit the essential element of selectivity uncommonly well and thereby furnish a good entrance into the subject.

Each of the cases under consideration directs us to a special element of selectivity. The story of the woman at the well, for example, shows how a counselor must never let himself become derailed in his quest for significant information. The Christian counselor, especially, is extremely vulnerable to the temptation that she placed before Jesus: the temptation to become sidetracked on a timely doctrinal issue. Here the temptation is to be lured away from a pursuit of the usual by a concern for the unique. The counselor must not give in to his own desires to set another straight doctrinally when the matter does not pertain to the problem at hand.[3] It is especially when the counselor gets close to a painful area and is about to strike oil (to change the metaphor) that a counselee may raise all sorts of interesting but unrelated and distracting issues. Theological questions like the one she asked are very tempting to the average pastor or Christian worker. Yet, he must not allow himself to be led off the main path by them. When a counselor discovers that a counselee suddenly shifts his/her interests and begins to raise all sorts of questions that have no relationship to the discussion that has been going on, he may well look for pay dirt in the area he has been probing. That is one good sign that he is on the right track.

Note how it all takes place in the biblical account. Jesus begins with a personal concern—the woman's need for the life-giving water of salvation (John 4:10). She doesn't understand and takes Him literally (vv. 11, 12). He explains the difference, still somewhat enigmatically (vv. 13, 14), and she becomes interested (v. 15). Then, having ascertained that she was an outcast because of her way of life,[4] Jesus puts His finger on her sin (vv. 16-18). But because what He is saying is much hotter than what she wants to handle at the moment, and because she recognizes His unique prophetic abilities, she turns the conversation to a doctrinal dispute between the Jews and the Samaritans, an issue about which a prophet ought to be interested (vv. 19,20). Jesus answers the question briefly, but in such a way that He is able to turn the issue again toward the need (vv. 21-26). All of this culminates in His insistence that she must put her trust in Him as the Messiah. Then, skillfully, he dodges the trap and (indeed) uses what might have deteriorated into an abstract, doctrinal discussion as a means of exposing her personal problem. The seeming digression is turned around as He exposes her need to become a true worshiper of the true God who is "looking for" such persons and who offers them the right to worship Him when they receive the forgiveness of sins through faith in His Messiah.

---

3. When major issues at hand have been dealt with, doctrinal matters can be handled at length.

4. Women did not normally go for water (1) alone, (2) at this hour. Jesus knows this and reasons from these facts to the conclusion. Here, He discovers the usual (her sin) from the unusual circumstances.

It is all too easy for a counselor to allow a counselee to distract him. But when he knows what he is looking for (that is, when he has biblical insight into sinful human nature) and knows what he wishes to accomplish (that is, he has insight into God's solutions to man's problems), he will be able to be selective in his concerns because he will also know what is extraneous and digressing. It is insight, therefore, that keeps him on the right track and off the wrong ones.

Distractions may not always be intentional, as they were in the instance of the woman at the well. The counselee may genuinely be taken up with material that to him, but not to the counselor, may seem extremely significant ("But you see, I was an only child"). As a result, he may not wish to speak about much else. But the counselor must not permit him to lead the discussion astray any more than Jesus did. He must be in charge of the interview. He must pursue the most direct course possible to obtain the data he knows are important and to strike the emphases he knows ought to be made.[5] Taking his cue from Jesus, he must learn to redirect irrelevant concerns to the important areas that he wishes to investigate. Creativity, working with insight, will be necessary in many such instances to find ways of using the counselee's interests and directing them into the proper channel. So, the principle of selective insight allows for no digression from crucial concerns but, rather, treats all digressions as stepping stones for reemphasizing these concerns.

Let us now consider selectivity at work in the case of the rich young ruler (Mark 10:17-22). There were many things that Jesus might have said to this respectable young man. But He didn't. The insight Jesus gained into his problem riveted His attention wholly on one fact—the man trusted a false concept of goodness that had to be exposed. In two thrusts he dealt with the problem:

---

5. Of course, before taking action to forestall digression, the counselor will give full consideration to the point that the counselee is making. Frequently, what a counselee considers important really is. The counselor must not make up his mind ahead of time as Job's comforters did. Indeed, exactly the opposite must be true. For more on this see *What about Nouthetic Counseling?* pp. 49ff. The Christian counselor selects his areas of concern not arbitrarily, as Job's counselors did, but out of the interplay of biblical principle with the extensive data he gathers (see *The Christian Counselor's Manual* on data gathering). And he knows what questions to ask and which answers are significant on the basis of biblically directed insight into human beings.

1. "Why do you call me good? Nobody is good except One—God."
2. "Go sell all you have. . . ."

Jesus was saying that the young man must acknowledge Him as God or stop calling Him good on some lesser basis.

What is the principle of selectivity that Jesus exhibited in this case? It is this: A test will often confirm an insight.

Selecting the common but fundamental error in the rich young ruler's thought and life structure (goodness = outward conformity to the law), He made it abundantly clear to him, and to all others who read the account, that he was not really good since he loved money more than he loved God. In directing him to sell all that he owned, to give the proceeds to the poor, and to follow Him, Jesus by one stroke made it absolutely clear that true goodness is deeper than the young man had supposed and that according to His definition of goodness he was not good at all; rather, he was an idolater (cf. Col. 3:5). And He was able to do both by giving him the directive to sell all that he owned.

Selectivity led to the use of a test that grew out of the insight that He had into the inner emptiness of the young man. The second principle, then, is this: Often a test will best demonstrate the truth of a supposed insight.

Leaving all else aside, the area of concern is singled out, a test is devised and administered, and the results are evaluated.[6] Of course, in this case the test helped the young man and others to learn the facts that Jesus already knew. His insight was keen enough not to need the test. With us, the test may also confirm or lead to the modification of a tentative conclusion on the part of the counselor as well.

The third case, the account of Nicodemus, points up a third principle of selectivity. Because Jesus "knew what was in human beings"[7] (John 2:25), He directly confronted Nicodemus with his personal need. When it becomes obvious that there is one and only one major problem—here Nicodemus' salvation—which overshadows everything else, and the counselee himself seems both aware of it and eager to solve it, there is little reason to linger on other subjects. Jesus didn't. He focused on the

---

6. Cf. also Gen. 22:1, 2, 12, where God discusses His test of Abraham.
7. A good description of insight.

usual rather than the unique features of the case because that is the place where the need lay. Jesus was not impressed by the authoritative character of Nicodemus' mission, with what the Pharisees whom he represented might think, or anything else in the tension-filled situation. Nothing was allowed to intrude upon Nicodemus' real need. Personal need became the determining factor in the confrontation.

Too often we permit the person's status, factors relating to consequences, etc., to become a significant determinant in the counseling context. Whenever that happens, rather than helping the individual involved, rather than bringing about the best consequences possible (the ones that God wants), we create problems in both areas. We should do what God wants us to do in the situation regardless of who the counselee is and what may happen to us. It should not matter whether we may be counseling the mayor of our town, a notable Christian personality, or even the President of the United States. The one thing in mind should be that "this is a needy human being to whom God has called me to minister." A counselor gets into trouble if he begins to think, "This is the *President.*" Whenever he looks at anything else (e.g., if Jesus had thought, "I'll have to be especially careful here; Nicodemus is a representative of the Pharisees, and whatever happens could have a lot to do with my relationship to them in the future"), he falters and fails to do his best. We should be no more careful in counseling the President than in counseling a bum off the street. Both are sinful, needy human beings. We minister for God; therefore we minister well to both because we minister to both *for Him.* Only when we are able to selectively clear away all such extrinsic matters can we give our best help to the person himself and minister most helpfully.

In John 9, Jesus first healed the blind man after smearing clay on his eyelids. He did no counseling at all at that time. It was only on a second occasion that He told him about the healing of the blindness of the heart. Why did he wait so long to speak with him when, in contrast, he was so direct (indeed, one might even say abrupt) with Nicodemus? Because the latter was aware of his need; the former was not.

The blind man did not have even a lingering hope for physical healing, let alone a healing of the heart. That is why Christ applied the clay to his eyes. Certainly, He needed no secondary element to effect the healing;

the clay did not heal. Rather, that clay was wholly for the benefit of the blind man. As the clay hung heavily on his eyelids, he must have thought, "If only I could wash away my blindness as I can wipe away this obstruction." Hope, long buried, welled up within him once more. Then, just as he dared to hope again, he heard Jesus' words, "Go wash. . . ."

Nicodemus had come as a representative of the Pharisees, possibly volunteering in order to have the opportunity to confront Christ personally. I say that because Jesus deals with him in both capacities (representatively and personally). He knew what was in Nicodemus. A major point in the account is Christ's great insight.[8] He *knew* that there was an empty, longing, weary, seeking, heart in the man, and He spoke to it.

Now, let's sum up a bit. Selectivity is important because it allows the counselor to strip away all those things that might keep him from focusing on the real issue or issues. It keeps him off sidetracks, it protects him from becoming apprehensive about consequences and allows him to test his judgments about the counselee. There is more to selectivity than this, but for now that is enough to point up its importance to the development of insight.

Christian counselors must always have in mind, "What is the basic problem here?" as they work with a counselee (of course, they will allow for more than one problem, and they will recognize the important fact that a complicating problem in time itself may have become basic). And, singing their mental round, at the same time, they also must ask, "What does God want the counselee to do about it?"

As they select the major problem, they will *note* secondary features (laying them aside temporarily is not ignoring them) that they expect to clear up once the major problem(s) is (are) solved. And at that time they will come back to them, examining each one to make sure that it was cleared up by what has been done. If any yet remains, it too must be dealt with. Now, think about this case:

---

8. John 2:25 is actually the beginning of the story of Nicodemus; the chapter heading breaks apart the continuity that appeared in the original Gospel. All chapter headings and versifications were added hundreds of years later and are not inspired.

A young, single woman, twenty-eight years of age, comes for counseling with complaints of meaninglessness and purposelessness. Early in the discussion the counselor says, "Ruth, why don't we talk for a little while about the fact that you are not yet married?"

What makes him take that approach? Why does he turn the conversation in that direction? Why doesn't he discuss the philosophical questions that she seems to be raising? Is he insensitive? Exactly the opposite.

By a few well-placed questions he confirms[9] his earlier suspicions, and in a kindly way asks his question. To others, with less insight, the change of direction may seem as abrupt and unwarranted as when Jesus turned the topic from His miracle-working to Nicodemus' personal need. But to the counselor and to Ruth, who may begin to wonder about his powers of insight, it is a correct turn that she eagerly acknowledges, as in response she pours out the burden of her problem with all of the anguish and bitterness that has been festering for so long. How did he know to do that? What is this mysterious thing called insight, anyway? He knew that he ought to ask Ruth this question because, like his Lord, he too "knows what is in a human being," though, of course, imperfectly and to a much lesser extent. That is insight. But how does he know? That sort of knowledge isn't innate. The answer to that question leads to the next chapter.[10]

---

9. But, note well, he does not counsel on suspicion, intuition, or according to stereotyped patterns. He may be alerted by any or all of these, but always *confirms* suppositions before reaching conclusions and acting on them.

10. Before turning the page, think about this matter and see if your conclusion agrees with the one suggested there.

3

COMMON PROBLEMS
AND THE COUNSELOR'S PAST

The counselor mentioned in the previous chapter asked Ruth about her single state because he *knew* that for unmarried women of her age singleness is often a serious problem. When she focused on meaninglessness and purposelessness, he also *knew* that these abstractions very readily could have been her way of telling him that the purposes she had been anticipating for sometime had not been realized and that as a consequence she now had begun to look at her life as meaningless. In the discussion that followed, he would take up those aspects of the problem, but it would have been totally wrong to discuss these abstract issues *per se* apart from the concrete matter that lay behind them. What may have seemed to Ruth like extraordinary insight on the counselor's part, however, was rather ordinary and, one might even say, routine.[1]

When I use words like ordinary and routine, what I am saying is that insight into particular situations may be greatly assisted by the results of past efforts. Indeed, without a counseling past, there can be no counseling insight at all. This past forms the *basis* of all insight.

Insight, in large measure, is the product of facts that one has learned in the past applied to similar situations as he confronts them in the present. Rarely, if ever, does a flash of absolutely fresh insight (i.e., insight unrelated to the past) appear on one's horizon like summer lightning. When it *seems* to do so to others, or even to the counselor himself, he is actually depending heavily on his past—even if he doesn't realize this. Fortunately, this takes much of the guesswork and a great deal of the mystery out of counseling.

Elders have been given the task of overseeing the church of the Lord Jesus Christ precisely for this reason—they are *elders* (i.e., "old men" or, better, "seasoned, mature" men; they are *men with a past* that can be used in shepherding the flock). Counseling, as a life calling, is the task of elders. But God calls all other Christians to counsel too.[1] Everyone has some sort of a past, not just elders.

---

1. Cf. my book, *Ready to Restore*.

"But, how can one use the results of a counseling past if in his past he has done no counseling? A person like that has no past to lean on. And, if a past is needed, how does a beginner ever get started? Isn't this the old dilemma where you need it to get it?" These are good questions. I should like to respond by suggesting that there are two possible answers:

1. He may stumble, err, and slowly learn, at the expense of a number of counselees, or
2. He may learn from the Scriptures and their use in the counseling experience of others; that is to say, he may "borrow" a past.

Most counselors rightly prefer to follow the second course of action. It is cruel and thoughtless to adopt the first course if it is not necessary to do so. The best way to learn is to watch a seasoned counselor at work as his disciple. Next best is to read what counselors have written. In order to share some of my own past, I have listed in the back of *The Christian Counselor's New Testament* some materials that, if learned, will give the beginning counselor a *basic* biblical "past." I shall reproduce it here and then make some comments on it.

Why People Come for Counseling

It is important to distinguish among the various problems that motivate persons to seek help. The following list, while not exhaustive, may aid. It includes twenty of the most frequent reasons why persons seek counselors.

1. Advice in making simple decisions
2. Answers to troublesome questions
3. Depression and guilt
4. Guidance in determining careers
5. Breakdowns
6. Crises
7. Failures
8. Grief
9. Bizarre behavior
10. Anxiety, worry, and fear
11. Other unpleasant feelings
12. Family and marital trouble

13. Help in resolution of conflicts with others
14. Deteriorating interpersonal relations
15. Drug and alcohol problems
16. Sexual difficulties
17. Perceptual distortions
18. Psychosomatic problems
19. Attempted suicide
20. Difficulties at work or school

It is important to know in what areas problems are likely to lie. With various classes of persons, special areas ordinarily (perhaps *usually*) contain the "hot spots."

With *children,* counselors should look for problems in child/parent relations, peer-group difficulties, and teacher and school tensions.

With *older children and singles,* in additon to some of the above, explore the possibility of sexual difficulties, dating problems, communication breakdown, trouble with life-meaning, the discovery, development and use of gifts, and school and/or work.

With *older singles,* look especially for resentment over failure to marry and explore objectionable habit patterns that may have become obstructions to and reduce one's marriage potential. Look for possible homosexual or lesbian problems. Check up on disorganization of life schedules.

With *married persons,* investigate not only strains arising from the marriage itself, but from the family's relationship to in-laws, problems relating to work or homemaking, financial worries, and the discipline of children. Communication breakdown, resentment, and depression are all possibilities too.

Older persons may suffer from loneliness, self-pity, physical aches and pains, time wastage, purposelessness, and the fear of death.

Handicapped persons also present specialized problems. In particular, look for resentment (against God and/or others), loneliness, and self-pity. A sense of uselessness may prevail. Such persons need to be shown how to thank God for problems and how to turn their liabilities into assets by the grace of God. Often the handicapped counselee has developed patterns in which he has learned to use his handicap to manipulate others around him.

Not all of these problems are always present in each case. In some instances the special factors that characterize an individual in a particular category may play no part in the problem at all. Yet, even where some other problem or problems not specifically related to age, or singleness, or marriage, etc., seem to dominate, the special problems within the category may form secondary or complicating problems (e.g., "I know why we had the argument; I'm old and useless and just in everyone's way"), and will have to be dealt with as well.

Now, it should be understood that these generalizations are just that, and nothing more.[2] That means they are broad, sweeping observations that quite frequently hold true and that will often put one on the main track or on a track that leads to it.[3] But, just as readily, if he allows them to do so, these generalizations may become a means of switching him onto a sidetrack. What I am saying is that the counselor's past, whether acquired from his own counseling experience or derived from the work of others, must never be considered absolute. It is one, basic factor; but only that. This means that the counselor must always be ready to have his best judgment and his tentative conclusions overturned partly or entirely. Unless he is willing to gather facts and allow the data gathered to push him in other, more correct directions, he will continually be going astray just as Job's counselors did.

No counselor knows all possible situations or combinations of factors. No counselor knows the Scriptures adequately enough to have just the right responses ready at all times. There is always more to learn. And even what has been learned often must be revised, updated or, in part or in the whole, scrapped. Biblical understanding *grows*. That growth, like the growth that takes place in your garden, can be cultivated, but it cannot be rushed or forced.

Because of sinful human limitations, *confirmation* of suppositions must be sought throughout the process. Confirmation does not mean

---

2. But they are *frequent*. Do not look for more exotic explanations until you are *very* sure that one or more of these doesn't cover the *basic* problem(s).

3. A counselor with mature insight will also know the most likely additional possibilities to check out in those unusual cases where the more usual observations do not prove correct. But in this book it would be going too deeply into matters to list them as well.

trying to prove that one is correct; rather, it means asking one's self what other possible explanations could be given for the phenomenon and testing one's suppositions to see if, in fact, they hold up under such scrutiny. Tests of one's conclusions are best conducted by giving homework based on the data gathered and the best tentative explanations of these data, which, by its accomplishment or failure, often will demonstrate the willingness of the counselee to work, his ability to perform a task, or the truth or falsehood of a supposition that has thus far been made.[4]

An assignment to keep a record of all the circumstances in which a counselee tends to become angry, for example, will help to confirm or to disprove a counselor's assumption (yet unrevealed to the counselee so it will not prejudice the results of the test) that it is always in stress situations that this happens.[5]

Even when confirmation takes place as the result of the gathering and testing of adequate evidence, the counselor still must avoid stereotyping. It is possible that although Ruth's problem is quite similar to Ellen's, and even when it is basically the same, there may be enough minor or secondary differences to require quite a different approach. So, if you dealt successfully with Ellen and closed her case last week, the particulars of Ruth's singleness problem may require solutions that are very different. How can this be?

Let us suppose that Ellen's problem was rather simple: a lack of exposure to men. Once the proper moves toward greater exposure were made, the problem went swimmingly on its way toward a solution. In Ellen's case, just to fill it out a bit, the exposure problem was linked to the false idea that she should pray and wait and do no more. ("God will send my future husband riding up on a white horse someday with a glass slipper in his hand that fits my foot alone," she kept telling herself in one form or another.) This is an idea that many Christian girls have, and the fact should be noted and stored with the rest of the material in the counselor's mental files that we have been calling his counseling *past*.

---

4. On data gathering and on homework, see appropriate sections in my book, *The Christian Counselor's Manual*.

5. Here, a DPP (discovering problem patterns) form will be found useful (cf. *The Manual*).

These girls fail to recognize that in the early church, contacts were made for young ladies by their fathers (cf. I Cor. 7:36ff.). Enlisting fathers today to take initiative on behalf of single daughters in whatever way they can is not out of the question, though this may call for some creative discussion by a counselor since the idea, doubtless, will be brand new to most Christian fathers. But what if someone objects that ''it just isn't done!'' There are a *number* of biblical things that aren't done and yet *ought* to be done. Until we start doing them, they won't be. Of course, prayer must precede and follow all that is done; I am by no means urging the neglect of prayer. Rather, I am urging prayer *plus* a use of all of the biblical means for effecting the result. God expects us to engage in both; not merely in one to the exclusion of the other.[6]

But now, let us return to Ruth. She too wants to be married, but her background is quite the opposite of Ellen's. Recently saved out of a scarlet past, Ruth now has sour attitudes toward men in general and distorted views on sex; she also has a bitterness toward *men*—not toward *God,* as Ellen did. Those differences call for a different approach and different solutions. And they are just as important to deal with before marriage as Ellen's problems were. Ruth hopes that Christian men will be different, but wonders whether her hopes are at all realistic. She wants to be married, but not to a man like those men she has known in the past. And to complicate matters, the few Christians she has dated so far proved no less immoral in their advances than her unsaved dates.

Clearly, then, though the basic area of concern (singleness) is the same for both Ellen and Ruth, the problems they face and, therefore, the solutions are almost altogether different. One is a problem of singleness *combined* with a problem of underexposure, while the other is a problem of singleness *combined* with patterns of sexual promiscuity. The problem of singleness is common to both, but the other problems are not; they are quite distinct. Each of these distinct problems, however, has its own common features. And it will be common to a competent biblical counselor.

Because of the differences that different combinations of problems bring about, it is a fatal mistake for any counselor to isolate only one

---

6. See the note at the end of this chapter.

factor. He must sort out the various strains of the counselee's problem and find the commonalities or ordinary features in each. Insight, leaning on what is ordinary and common, then, has to do with each ordinary feature in a case at each level.

It would have been the height of folly for a counselor to take the same course with Ruth as he took with Ellen simply because they both had *one* factor in common. At the outset, there was a basic congruity between the cases—both were seeking a husband. That common factor in their responses led to that common conclusion. But having examined the details of each case carefully, the competent counselor would soon conclude that further resemblances between the cases were few and far between. The past proved a valuable tool to move past step one to step two, but having done so, in each case the counselor was forced to look at entirely different sub-areas in his counseling past. Counselors with rich pasts will possess biblical and biblically derived materials dealing with most of the possible sub-categories within each general area. Yet, even there, where they will discover extensive overlapping, they will also find significant differences. Some of these differences come from differing combinations of problems; others come from different wrappings and packaging or from different complicating problems. Because no two persons and no two situations are ever exactly the same, there is *always* a need for a creative handling of each case. That is to say, despite all of the similarities that appear, in the final analysis no persons may ever be treated routinely. There may be routine solutions and routine homework assignments growing out of these at some points, but never is it possible to use *only* a routine approach to a human being. There is always a need for creativity. Every case demands it, and that is why this book is not concerned with insight alone.

In addition to these generalizations about classes of counselees there are a number of other generalizations about counselees as a whole that enable a counselor to gain insight. In order to demonstrate the sort of thing I have in mind, I shall briefly mention seven complicating problems that many counselees may have, in addition to other major problems.[7]

---

7. Of course, any one of or any combination of these problems also may constitute a major problem or may become such when not dealt with properly in counseling.

1. *Lack of Discipline*

Perhaps the greatest overall complicating problem that counselors encounter is lack of discipline.[8] Wise counselors, i.e., counselors with a past, either borrowed or acquired on their own (no biblical counselor ever actually acquires a past strictly on his own, since the foundation for all that he does must come from the Scriptures[9]), know in every case to look for the presence of this complicating factor in addition to others they may encounter. They also have studied carefully the subject of discipline and thought much about it, so that they are prepared at all times to help counselees with this common problem.

Bill needs to get control of his mind in accordance with God's biblical leash law found in Philippians 4:8. He now allows it to roam all over the neighborhood, rummaging in any garbage can in sight. But he will never do so without discipline. Mary has a problem with her tongue; it violates all of the passages in Proverbs and in James. But apart from biblical discipline, she will never succeed in controlling it. So you can see, the common problems are not simply mind control and tongue control, but rather, they are mind-discipline and tongue-discipline problems. These are combination problems.[10] Unless the counselor sees them as such, he is more likely to fail his counselee than not.

2. *Lack of Creative Imagination*

Because I shall discuss this matter at great length later in the book, I shall say little here about creativity in counseling beyond noting that apart from the ability to translate biblical principles into how-to implementation that snugly fits the particulars of each counselee's case,

---

8. On discipline and how to achieve it, see my book, *Ready to Restore*. A useful help in working with counselees is my handout pamphlet, *Godliness through Discipline*. The devotional workbook, *Four Weeks with God and Your Neighbor*, was designed, in part, to afford a plan for achieving discipline.

9. The counselor who knows well the Book of Proverbs, for instance, is a counselor with a past. Here he has, in his possession, the inspired and inerrant wisdom of God, compiled in a thoroughly down-to-earth style by experienced men of God, on a variety of life problems. No counselor can afford to counsel apart from a thorough and continued study of this book.

10. Of course, there can be other problems mixed in too; especially problems of heart and attitude.

those principles remain abstract and impractical and actually become discouraging to the counselee because, in that form, they cannot be followed, even when the counselee wants to follow them. Creativity is needed for accomplishing anything new. Change is new. If the counselee lacks creativity—and a great number of counselees do—initially the counselor must supply creatively adapted biblical solutions, and then he must teach the counselee himself how to go about acquiring and using a measure of creativity in the future implementation of biblical principles.

Contrary to what some may think, insight that uncovers the need for creativity and the need for teaching creativity is not something remarkable for the counselor with a past; as a matter of fact, it has always been quite a routine concern of biblical counselors. However, the terms *insight* and *creativity* themselves may be new to them. Biblical counselors have had little to say about these activities even though they have been involved in them. What is new is that I have labeled these activities. Getting a label for what one is already doing tends to sharpen the activity, gives one a more thorough grasp of what it involves, and provides items for one's counseling check list. [11] It is my hope that this book will go a long way toward doing just those things for biblical counselors who are concerned about improving their counseling.

3. Lack of Commitment

Constantly in Christian literature we read about commitment, but no one ever seems to spell out exactly what is meant by the term. As I see the word used in various places, there seem to be four essential ingredients: understanding, agreement, desire, and responsibility. A person is not truly committed to a biblical change unless he fully *understands* the differences between the past practice and the new one (in biblical terms), *agrees* that this change is right (often this agreement stems only from repentance), *desires* to see the change take place in order to please God (other priorities can take second or third place behind this one, but this always must be first), and is willing to assume the *responsibility* for doing all that God requires and enables him to do to bring it about. Apart

---

11. For more on the importance—and the dangers—of labeling in counseling, see my book, *The Language of Counseling.*

from a basic commitment that includes all of the factors just mentioned, counseling will fail. It can go bad by neglecting even one of them. Counselees often lack necessary commitment because they lack one or two of the four factors; all four must be present. There can be no proper commitment by persons who have no idea what they are committing themselves to, who, even if they understand, are forced against their wills to do it, who do it for unbiblical reasons, or who want the right results but not enough to assume the responsibility to make the efforts that will bring them about.

4. A Lack of Perseverance

All too often there is a willingness on the part of the counselee to settle for too little too soon. As soon as the pain has been removed many counselees want to discontinue counseling. This poses a new problem for the counselor. As much as he may wish to accede to their wish, he must forestall this possibility. Until the counselee has fully learned

(1) the biblical explanation of how he got into his problem,
(2) the biblical dynamic by which he got out of it in counseling,
(3) how to avoid getting into the problem again in the future, and
(4) what to do if he should happen to get into it again,

he is not ready to be dismissed from counseling.

Moreover, the counselee must have put on new biblical patterns in the place of the old sinful ones, or be well on his way toward doing so, and he must be restored to his place of useful activity in Christ's church, before the termination of counseling is indicated. Other matters may prolong the sessions from the usual 4-8 weeks to 10 or even 12. But counselors must insist on continuation, explaining why, whenever it is for the benefit of the counselee to do so. For more on the termination of counseling, see my book, *Ready to Restore: A Layman's Guide to Counseling*.

5. Lack of Personal Accountability

From Eden on, people have been blaming others for their own sins. Another important element, then, that is needed for developing insight is the ability to recognize and identify blame-shifting. So long as counselees are permitted to excuse their transgressions by shifting responsibility to others, counseling will falter.

Sorting out the responsibilities of counselees, therefore, can be one of the most significant skills for a counselor to learn if he wishes to excel in exercising insight.[12] The counselor who knows how to do this well, and who practices it regularly throughout all his counseling sessions, will do very well in counseling and will find that early in most cases he is headed on the right track. Those who fail to sort out and assign responsibilities are doomed to take many wrong paths and will find themselves and their counselees continually lost in the woods.

"Yes, Bill," you will hear a biblical counselor saying, "I know that it was after Mary said what she did that you responded that way, but while she sinned in saying that, nevertheless you sinned in storming out of the house and smashing the glass door. She is responsible for *her* nasty words, but you are responsible for *your* words and violent actions. You should have responded righteously to her wrongdoing. Mary, you could have said something entirely different in the first place; your words were a stumbling block. But Bill was responsible to watch his step and not trip over it. Both of you will have to learn how to do whatever it is that pleases God, regardless of what anyone else may say or do. The Lord Jesus didn't storm out of the house when someone failed to accept His teaching. When people wronged Him, He always, in response, did the right thing (i.e., the thing that pleased God, and which, therefore, also was the best for them). His words and actions were determined by His desire to please God, not by what someone else may have said or done to Him. Now, Mary, let's talk about what you could have said to Bill in the first place instead of the words that occasioned this row. . . ."

6. *Lack of Biblical Objectives*

When a counselee says, "I'll do anything to hold on to my job," or words to that effect, I am always suspicious of his agenda. His own words create the suspicion. (I Cor. 13 indicates that it is not right to

---

12. Sometimes the ability to identify and assign responsibilities according to biblical principles is itself considered by counselees to be great insight because this way of thinking is so foreign to their own.

become suspicious apart from evidence.)[13] I then usually ask him, "Anything?" Do you really mean that? Would you lie? Would you vilify another employee?"

"Well, no. . . ."

"Then tell me, just what would you do?"

"I guess I really don't know."

"Then it seems important for us to talk about your counseling agenda, don't you think? After all, we want to be sure about your objectives; they must line up with God's objectives or everything will go wrong. What you *should* say (and mean) is 'I'll do anything God wants me to about my problem.' That means that your first priority must be to please God, not to hold on to your job or anything else. If you do what *He* requires of you in the situation, then you will succeed whether you keep your job or not. And if you lose your job, only then will you be in a condition to handle that contingency. If you retain it, you'll be in a better position than ever to make a success of it too. Whichever way you go, if your first priority is to please God in the situation, you will be right. Any other set of priorities will automatically cause you to fail in His sight, even if you happen to succeed in your own mind and in the eyes of men."

Often, agendas must be renegotiated with counselees. Because we know that sinners (even saved ones) are selfish and that most will revert to selfishness in times of trouble, even if they have been outwardly thoughtful of others when things are going well, it is no great matter to suppose that self-centered, rather than God-centered concerns will appear on their agendas. So objectives and priorities are a matter of insight in counseling that we certainly must not forget. Such a discussion of goals and objectives at the outset of any counseling case where they are in doubt can open counseling quickly, as few other factors could. Evaluation of agendas is routine because so many counselees come with problems in this area. Insight, then, is a matter of knowing where to locate which problems and, as a result, going right after them as soon as the supposition that such problems exist is confirmed. Probing for the lack of biblical objectives is routine.

---

13. See *Update on Christian Counseling*, vol. II, for an exposition of I Cor. 13 in relation to counseling.

7. Lack of Commandment-orientation

For more than two generations the Western world has been inundated with advertising, literature, and ideologies that appeal to the gratification of feelings. The hedonistic philosophy of modern humanism that prevails may be summed up most succinctly in the bumper sticker that reads, "If it feels good, do it." Concurrently, psychiatrists and psychologists by the droves have been inculcating not only the idea that one ought to follow his feelings but also that he should freely express them and that it is "unhealthy" to say "no" to feelings. Many of these persons, while meaning well and seeking to help others who are in trouble, advocate these feeling-oriented solutions, not recognizing that (at least in part) it is the following of feelings that has led to the trouble in the first place. While it is not necessary for a counselee to have counseled with a hedonistic counselor to have acquired a feeling orientation toward life—his whole culture is permeated with it—those who have been to a psychiatrist or psychologist before should be questioned especially about any feeling-oriented "solutions" that were recommended and that, if followed, may have complicated matters.

As a result of the strong emphasis on feelings in our society, nearly all counselees suffer to some extent (often to a large extent) from their orientation toward feeling-motivation. All, therefore, must be taught, in contrast, that they must follow God's commands and the responsibilities that these lay upon them rather than their feelings, and they must do so *whether they feel like it or not.* Jesus Christ did not feel like going to the cross, but He did so in spite of His feelings.

Again, knowing this fact provides insight. And finding the feeling-orientation problem in a counselee again is no great surprise to a biblical counselor; he looks for it. It is routine to do so. That is to say, it is an insight that he possesses into sinful human nature as a result of his counseling "past."[14] What I hope that these seven examples of generalizations (by no means an exhaustive list), together with the list of problems related to special classes of persons and the comments and

---

14. For more on these seven points, the biblical data underlying them, and what to do about them, see the indexes of my other books. For a full list of books, write C.S.S., 2435 Oak Circle, Huntington Valley, PA 19006, and a catalog will be sent to you.

observations about insight, will do for you is to remove the mystery from insight. There is nothing at all mysterious or esoteric about insight in biblical counseling; it is an ordinary process that is constantly at work whenever effective biblical counselors draw on their knowledge of counselees. This knowledge, we have seen, is the counselor's *past*. It is derived from biblical principles and examples that they have used, observed others use, or read about others using concretely in the lives of counselees.

Ordinarily, one does not suddenly see everything clearly in a flash of insight if he has no past. It is true that the discovery of a major problem, the ability to distinguish between things that differ or capability to penetrate into the depths of an issue may come suddenly. But when it does, you can count on the fact that this happens because the sorts of processes that I have been describing have been at work. Use of the counselor's past has been involved (perhaps unconsciously). It is not that the counselor has had some sort of inspiration out of the blue; human minds do not operate in a void. Insight is the judicious use of the ordinary and the routine. That, in a nutshell, is the principal insight into insight. Insight is the inevitable result of a counseling past that is coupled with good counseling practice. It is like the expert diagnosis of a physician who has studied the literature thoroughly and examined enough patients to know what to look for and what his findings mean.

Far from being something special, unique, or unusual then, the presence of insight in a counselor indicates that he is in touch with the ordinary, the routine, and the usual. He, too, knows what is in people. His study of the Scriptures and their application to human life is broad and accurate. For him, insight is a matter of looking for and finding the factors (or combinations of them) that he already knows are there. What he does not know until he has gathered the data that will tell him, is which of the ordinary, usual problems are present, and in what combinations. It is safe to say that there is no case that does not manifest at least one or more of these common problems. Indeed, it is often true that all seven will appear. As a result of his knowledge about them, a competent counselor experiences fewer and fewer surprises.

All counselors are fallible and growing. That is why, at times, all of them are taken by surprise. They must constantly study, learn, and use their learning, so that the surprises will be fewer and fewer and their insight will grow wider still. The number of surprises that a counselor runs into may be one index of the amount of insight that he possesses. (See the Appendix for help in this matter.)

Contrary to the views of many, insight is nothing more or less than working with the ordinary.[15] The counselor with insight surprises others because he himself is so seldom surprised. The average person does not possess the past that he has and cannot be expected to understand how he reaches his conclusions. But the competent counselor is able to penetrate to the deepest layers of the problem because he knows how to distinguish the ordinary from the unusual.

What is unusual, an experienced counselor knows, is almost always not basic to the problem, and may be eliminated or, at least, temporarily laid aside (for more on this see the next chapter). Inexperienced counselors, even when they have acquired a past by borrowing, have a tendency to focus on the unusual and the unique rather than to look for the ordinary. This is one reason why they so often fail to gain the insight that is needed. They allow unusual features to frighten them or, on the other hand, to so allure them that they focus their attention on these factors rather than on the ones that count.

NOTE

After you have read the section on creativity, turn to page 28 and list ten possible ways for fathers to help single daughters to become exposed to the right sorts of men. Be sure all of these suggestions are biblically legitimate.

---

15. The question may be asked: "Isn't the unusual often what gives away the nature of a person's problem? If a person begins to talk about hearing voices. . . ." Yes, but you are speaking about that which is unusual *for the counselee* (he has never heard voices before); I have been talking about what is usual or unusual *to the counselor*. For the counselor, bizarre behavior is one *usual* clue to a problem and/or its possible sources.

1. _____
_____
_____

2. _____
_____
_____

3. _____
_____
_____

4. _____
_____
_____

5. _____
_____
_____

6. _____
_____
_____

7. _____
_____
_____

8. _____
_____
_____

9. _____
_____
_____

10. _____
_____
_____

4

WHAT TO ELIMINATE

I said at the conclusion of the previous chapter that an experienced biblical counselor knows how to eliminate the unusual as he seeks to discover the essential, ordinary factors that lie behind the counselee's difficulties; inexperienced counselors, on the other hand, tend to get tangled up in the unusual features of a case, thereby missing the fundamental dynamics that are at work. The operative problems, generally speaking, are the *ordinary* ones, not the unique ones. Because this is true, it is important to know something about what the unusual *usually* looks like. In other words, we must try to make the elimination of non-essential, unusual factors also a matter of routine.

If insight is the ability to isolate and identify the usual, and if an important step in that process is the elimination of extraneous factors, then what one needs to know as a part of his counseling past is what sorts of unusual problems usually should be bypassed. These eliminated matters may, of course, have significance for other purposes. But for the purpose of discovering precisely what a counselee's problem is and precisely what God wants done about it, elimination of all that is not directly pertinent to that matter is essential.

The information in the following ten categories may help you to avoid misleading and diversionary avenues. In looking for the usual beneath the unusual, eliminate the following:

1. *Psychiatric and psychological jargon* together with the humanistic interpretations and ideas that lie behind it. Because I have written so fully about the errors of psychotherapy in a number of books, and because of the non-polemical nature of this book, I shall not elaborate on this matter here. Let it be sufficient to say that the counselor may ignore almost all interpretations stemming from such categories. Typically these interpretations cloud rather than illuminate problematic situations. There may be significance, however, in a counselee's excessive use of such terminol-

ogy or in any obvious dependence by him upon psychotherapeutic notions if these have become the justification for sinful behavior or he has bought into one of these many systems and is trying to follow it. If complicating problems have grown out of attempts to do so, this fact could be of importance.

However, the use of jargon, or even the interpretation of events in psychotherapeutic lingo by counselees, ordinarily should not be considered of much significance. Such terminology has become the possession of the ordinary man or woman in the street, and, for some reason, many counselees think that they can be of help to the counselor by using it. They will say things like, "I think I've got a guilt complex," when what they really mean is, "I'm guilty and I feel lousy about it." They will tell you, "I guess that's due to my feelings of inferiority," or other words to the same effect, when they have little idea about what such words mean. Some counselors are awed by the use of this terminology; don't be. It is ordinarily good practice just to ignore it altogether when gathering data, or it will prejudice, rather than help, as you attempt to interpret the situation by it.

2. *Guesses and speculation* on the part of the counselee should be eliminated regularly. Unless the guesses are "educated" guesses—i.e., they are based on facts and evidence—forget them. When a counselee guesses, ask, "On what evidence do you base that supposition?" The answer to that question will help you to distinguish a guess from an "educated" guess. Asking that question consistently and often of a counselee who is inclined to speculate also will soon reduce the amount of speculation that he does in counseling and will lead him to concentrate more on factual information.

3. *Victim themes* do not yield information about facts, though they do tell you something about the counselee who may rely on them to manipulate others or to justify failure and sin. Except for the purpose of exposing these sinful purposes, ignore such contentions as "Mother did it to me" (in whichever of the dozen or more forms this excuse may appear), "society did it to me" (in either its tear-jerking or its belligerent form), and "the devil did it to me" (appearing fully robed in garbs of pious, hypocritical religiosity). No one else can make another person sin by what he does to him. Keeping that fact in mind, the competent,

biblical counselor will bypass such misleading pathways. Of course, he may need to refute them with biblical counter-teaching if the counselee is truly depending on such dodges for refuge. But as information-gathering pathways to pursue, they are all but useless.

4. *Blame-shifting ideas* have already been explored in the previous chapter. I shall not say more about them here except to note that all three of the victim themes just mentioned, plus others, can be changed, with only a slight alteration, into blame-shifting excuses: "Mother (society, my wife, the devil) *made* me do it." See also the next chapter for more on blame-shifting.

5. *Repetitive material,* that covers substantially the same ground with no additions or corrections, should be quickly swept aside, or probed for new data growing out of it (later on, under creativity, I shall say more about useful repetition). Some counselees repeat the same thing over and over again, if you allow them to do so. Useless repetition must be discouraged. But always do so in such a way that you make the counselee realize that you welcome repetition that covers new material. Few things can be as unproductive as taking a trip in a revolving door. Learn to help the counselee to move out and on.

6. *Unnecessary or unrelated details, eddies, and sidetracks* are also to be eliminated from consideration. Although details can be of great significance, the experienced counselor knows how to distinguish between these and the gallons of meaningless details that some counselees pour forth. Some of these people are social bores who have lost the ear of others largely because they talk constantly about themselves and make all sorts of mountains out of insignificant molehills. Now that they have the willing ear of a counselor, they exploit this opportunity to talk about *themselves* and to bring you up to date on the trivialities of their lives for the past 30 years. But, again, I warn you; be careful here. A seemingly irrelevant detail, carefully probed, may yield valuable information even from the inveterate talker. Because he ranges so far and wide, he is likely to say things that, when properly explored, may be used in determining the true facts of the counseling situation. In this category of unnecessary details also fall most of the unusual, glaring, or gaudy surface features that are so tempting for a counselor to pursue.

7. *Complaints, grumbling,* etc., must be eliminated in the data-

gathering process. However, note of grumbling and complaining attitudes should be made, and at the appropriate time the counselee must be confronted about his attitudes. But, unless the complaint is justified and bears directly on the issue at hand, it will be of little help in gaining insight into the counseling problem other than making you wonder whether by his attitude the grumbler may have given occasion for difficulty or enlarged a problem that otherwise might have been solved rather easily.

8. *Self-pity, sympathy-soliciting, and tear-jerking comments or actions* must be set aside. These can greatly obscure the truth as a counselee, allowed to turn the session into a pity party, will concentrate on his feelings rather than relate facts. At the right time, it is also necessary to deal with such behavior. Be careful here; at times true sorrow and grief may be mistaken for theatrical exhibitions. If there is a doubt, give the benefit of it to the counselee. True sorrowing persons may find that their genuine feelings get in the way, but under most circumstances they can be helped by a sensitive counselor to reveal needed data anyway.

9. *Questions asked by the counselee* that distract from data-gathering (whether they were intended to do so or not) can get you so far off the track that you may never find your way back. The way to handle these is to make a note of them on your Weekly Record Sheet under the Agenda column (see the *Manual* for details on the WRS) and postpone discussion until a more appropriate time. Counselees who mean business usually will be willing to wait; others may not. Either way, the possible distraction will be diverted.

10. *Structure that may limit, prejudice or impede* further investigation must be avoided. ''Pastor, I am only concerned about two things. . . .'' The counselor must be in charge of the counseling session, and while the counselee's intentions in structuring the investigation may be entirely honorable, the counselor may not allow him to curtail important questioning or discussion.

These ten areas are by no means exhaustive, but serve as examples of the sorts of factors that must be eliminated in order to focus on the significant matters in a counseling case.

Of course, there is another factor that sometimes arises in a counseling case that may give to it the sort of secondary features that could cause a counselor to become diverted from the correct path—the glaringly unusual feature. I have already said something about this in chapter 2. For now, let me say simply this: it is important to know what to bypass in the search for the essential facts in a counseling case. When a counselor, like a physician, knows what to eliminate in making his diagnosis, he will find that this ability will take him a long way toward helping to penetrate quickly through surface data toward an accurate understanding of the problem at hand.

5

BIAS, TENTATIVENESS, AND INSIGHT

It is possible to make mistakes in identifying and in selecting the broad, usual causes of problems. Having a counseling past (acquired by personal counseling experience or vicariously through others who have shared their experience with you) will in large measure overcome this difficulty. However, there is one problem that itself grows out of too great a dependence on the counseling past.

Some would-be counselors, rather than using their past wisely, depend on it in a rigid, almost mechanical way. Lists of the sort that I have given, for example, are absolutized, and *every* case, whether it does or not, is *made* to fit into the various categories found in them.

Having a counseling past, to put it another way, means knowing what to look for. It also means knowing how to find it, and it means knowing what to eliminate because it is of no immediate significance. Without such a past, no counselor could counsel. But when you "know" what to look for, the danger is in *finding* it—even when it isn't there (or, at best, when what you discover isn't integral to the dynamics of the case). As a result, counselors who do not guard against this danger end up forcing the data to fit their preconceived ideas about the case. That is why I have already urged the counselor to be careful to *confirm* his findings through homework, tests, etc. Let me reemphasize the point by urging that you do so *every* time, even in those "open and shut" cases.

Freud, and the Freudians, have been notorious for violating this rule. Indeed, the Freudian system is designed to find exactly what the psychoanalyst expects to find, and safeguards against finding anything else are built in at every point. It is amazing to the uninitiated how Freudians regularly find oedipal complexes, fixations, etc. The Freudian also "knows" what the problems are beforehand and, sure enough, they turn out every time to be exactly what he expected—whether the counselee is helped by this finding or not. When an interpretation is given, a counselee may object to it. Never mind. The objection itself is seen, not as a

34

rational disagreement that ought to be weighed, but rather, as resistance —further evidence that the analyst is on the right track. Disagreement, therefore, only confirms the analysis for the psychotherapist. On that basis, you can see that the counselee never has a chance. And, incidentally, the system also keeps the "therapist" himself in the dark about the truth; he never has a chance to deviate either.

Obviously, this whole area is a tricky one. While every counselor must have a good idea (or two; having more than one possibility in mind helps) of what *could* be involved in a given case, he must be very careful to remain tentative about the matter until the data force him (not the other way round) to reach that or some other conclusion. Otherwise, he runs the danger of approaching a counselee as the Freudians do or as Job's counselors did.

Job's counselors came with a rigid, standard, unbiblical interpretation already formulated, into which they then tried to fit Job. When Job protested that the suit was too small, instead of trying it on for size they kept insisting that it was exactly the size he needed and thus would be a perfect fit. Their frustration is seen throughout the book as they unsuccessfully attempted to get Job to wear it. When he refused to admit to the inadequate theological notions that they had preconceived, they could do nothing more than rail at him. They were wrong and could not help Job because they came with their minds already made up; that was why they did not even bother to gather data. Others, like them, do the same thing today. Sometimes they go through the motions of gathering data; but when they do, the data never get a chance because of the iron-clad interpretations that are immediately clamped onto them.

More subtle than Job's counselors are those who gather data selectively (ignoring what doesn't fit their preconceived notions) and who distort or misshape the data that are impossible for them to ignore. So, you can see that the problem of bias is as important in counseling as it is anywhere else.

We can never remove ourselves from all bias; were it possible, it would be a mistake. A Christian must never lose his bias toward God and toward His truth. He must be willing to interpret all facts in the light of the Scriptures. Because it is impossible to separate one's bias from what he does, it is important to have the right bias—a biblical bias. But, the biblical bias itself is clear about one thing: man has been affected in all his nature by sin and is not to be trusted implicitly. That means his mind and all of his thinking in general have been adversely affected as well as every other aspect of his person. He will make mistakes because he is a sinner. Christians do not place great faith in sinful human nature. Unlike humanists, they believe in depravity enough to question whatever conclusions a human being may reach on his own—about anything. When Christians, whose minds are being renewed, are at their best, they therefore bring a questioning biblical bias to human conclusions—even to their *own* best conclusions. While they do not question God or His Word, they may well question their own interpretations of the Bible and their application of its truths to a particular counseling case.

In counseling, then, Christians know that it is important to be tentative about *what* biblical factor may be operative until all of the facts are in and have been studied prayerfully and carefully against the biblical data to determine the dynamics involved. The biblical bias that informs us about sinful, human activity is essential, but one must be careful within its framework not to decide too quickly which of the various biblical options, or which combinations thereof, are in fact operative in any given case.

While not all problems that a counselor is called upon to deal with are the result of sinful behavior by the counselee, a large number (perhaps the majority) are. Here we shall treat only those that have the counselee's sin at their base. And, because there is such a great variety of ways in which a counselee can get himself into trouble by sinning, we shall look, for a time, into only one: the ways that a counselee can respond wrongly when he is put on the spot about his sin.

I shall mention several different responses that, as such, or in combinations thereof, are very common. As always in developing insight, one must be concerned about the usual. Counselors look for these responses. But, until all of the data are in, it would be wrong to make anything more than a preliminary or tentative judgment about which, if any, is present in a given case.

Now, let's see how, by tentativeness, we may overcome the dangers of bias. Let's take, as an example, an area in which the danger readily appears. Because it is an important area to know about, I can teach it at the same time we focus on avoiding bias that distorts. For the sake of brevity in the present discussion, then, we shall confine our discussion to the four important responses made by Adam and Eve when they were confronted by God about their sin:

1. Adam tried to run from God's presence (Gen. 3:8);
2. Adam tried to hide from God's sight (Gen. 3:8);
3. Adam tried to cover his sin (Gen. 3:7);
4. Adam tried to shift the blame to God and to Eve (Gen. 3:12).
   Eve also did all of those things.

Every competent counselor regularly looks for these four sinful responses which, unfortunately, separately or in various combinations have continued to form the principal escapes for sinners ever since Eden. By running, covering, hiding, and blame-shifting, sinners throughout history have attempted to avoid personal responsibility for their sins. These responses are man's sinful substitutes for confession and repentance.

Of course, over the years sinners have refined their sinful ways of responding. Just as in modern warfare people no longer club one another to death but hurl sophisticated missiles instead, so hiding, running, etc., may take many forms, some of which are not physical at all. Yet it is the same sinful heart that does both. But when all of the sophistication is boiled off, what we are left with is the bare essentials: the four responses listed above. In fact, most (I would like to say all, but I am not sure about this[1]) sinful responses could be fairly described as running, covering, hiding, or blame-shifting, or as various combinations thereof.

Sometimes a counselor will discover that patterns of running dominate a counselee's life. He runs from jobs, from wives, from churches, from communities. Typically, when the counselor sees him, he has run up a blind alley and his back is against the wall. He has come to a point where there is no place left to run. He is out of resources. All that he has run from has finally caught up with him and is headed his way down the alley. He wants to flee again—that's his pattern—but his way is blocked. He is desperate, needs direction, and, at that point, usually is ready to listen to *any* way out. Therein lies the danger: taking advice as a gimmick

---

1. The study and resolution of this question would be a valuable contribution to counseling theory.

to get himself out of the alley. Instead, he must rewrite his agenda, and he must learn to face his obligations. The problem will be to bring him to repentance and to help him to begin a new way of life rather than offering him what he is likely to interpret (or to distort) as an escape from the alley—a new way to run.

Look quickly at the other three substitutes for repentance. Sometimes the counselor will find that a counselee is *hiding* in forests of activities, behind mounds of papers, or other busy work. In other cases, counselees will be discovered who have carefully *covered* their sin with specious arguments. Typically, they will be found wearing camouflaged clothing fashioned from fibers of lies, excuses, and other synthetic materials. Other counselees will respond, "Well, I would have done what I was supposed to do if so and so had only . . . ," *placing the blame* for failure at the foot of another, claiming that he is the saboteur behind it. Still others will put it the other way around: "I wouldn't have said that if she hadn't first. . . ." Whichever way the counselee has patterned his life, a counselor with insight will readily be able to "see" the four patterns (or some combination of them) at work.

Because these patterns are common, usual, counselors rightly look for them. But they will not conclude too quickly, "He's running from problems," simply from the fact that Joe has recently left a job (or even a second job). In certain cases, leaving a job may be prudent, and in others, the only action a Christian could conscientiously take. Until the evidence of a *pattern* of running (a succession of similar incidents, under similar conditions growing out of similar motives and circumstances) is in, it would be wrong to make that judgment. When he learns that Joe has left a job, however, he may *wonder,* "Could there be a pattern here?" and begin to ask questions calculated to confirm or disconfirm the idea. But it will be only *an idea held tentatively.*

It is not wrong to investigate thoroughly the *possibility* of the existence of a pattern. Thorough checking of the evidence alone can confirm *or disconfirm* that possibility. The checking process itself, therefore, is as non-biased as possible, attempting to follow the evidence, and counselors should make this clear to counselees as they begin. Indeed, the checking has, as one objective, the purpose of eliminating wrong bias. If that is plain, the counselee should appreciate the thoroughness of the approach and should cooperate. Sometimes, when the intent is not clear to a counselee, he wonders about what the counselor is up to: "Does he think that I have been avoiding responsibilities . . . ?" It is always important to be candid about what is going on whenever there could be any possibility of being misunderstood. Tell him the *two* purposes of checking.

But even when a counselor discovers that a running problem is present, he must still be thorough; he must still keep probing to see whether the pattern is simple or complex. It is possible that any one of or all of the other three patterns are also more or less present. After all, in the case of Adam and Eve, that was the case: all four were present. Certainly, to some extent each of the four is bound up in the other three. But which, if any, is dominant? Or is there a pattern where one is dominant? Probing will be necessary to find out about covering, running, and hiding. Blame-shifting and excuse-making (which is often a part of hiding too) usually will appear without much probing as the counselee tells his story, as he explains actions, and in his conversation in general.

From the very outset, experienced counselors begin to take notes of every significant statement that might be evidence of patterns (exact quotations of the pith of the statement are best). From these notes, they can draw conclusions, and later on, when the fact seemingly has been established, they can read them back to any counselee who may doubt the judgment. Many counselees do not recognize what they have been doing until confronted with evidence out of their own mouths. Even then, however, the counselor must allow the counselee to evaluate the evidence his way: "Well, you have heard what the evidence seems to indicate; how do you see it?" From his acceptance, his doubt, his denial, the counselor will be able to determine what the next step will be. And, of course, the counselee may possibly come up with an explanation that is quite different from the one you have reached, and with which you might concur once you have discussed it. We are not Freudians. It is wrong, therefore, to reach conclusions too hastily, as I am afraid some biblically oriented counselors do.

My plea, then, is for the biblical counselor to be careful, thorough, cautious, and tentative, putting his emphasis on the gathering of facts and their careful evaluation. Insight is not a matter of shaking conclusions out of one's sleeve; it is the pursuit of the usual, which takes many and varied forms. But insight also requires of those who seek it the acquisition of skills in data gathering[2] and evaluation, not merely a knowledge of the usual. A significant element in this evaluation process, we have seen, is a conscious, careful handling of bias. These skills must be developed until they are a part of the usual repertory and practice of the counselor. Conclusions are reached, not because the counselor has a magic wand to wave but because he knows *what* to look for and *how* to look for it.

Because every counselor will tend to find what he is looking for, it is very important for the Christian counselor to look for those things which the Scriptures describe as a part of sinful human nature and which, therefore, will be the ordinary and usual patterns that he discovers. That bias is good. But he must be careful to avoid all harmful and misleading personal bias as he does so.

---

2. For detailed discussion of data gathering, consult the *Manual*.

6

FOUR CONSIDERATIONS

It is possible for a counselor to become cocky about his ability to exercise insight; competent Christian counselors are subject to the temptation perhaps more than others because of their high rate of successful counseling experiences. Just about the time when one tends to fall into this trap, the Lord in mercy often throws him a curve: a case comes along that is so difficult, so different or so disturbing that he is humbled by it and is driven back to the Book once again in prayerful research. Every counselor needs humility; therefore, every counselor needs to fail.

But, along the way, there are other factors that may cause difficulties for any counselor as he tries to work insightfully with the ordinary and the usual. These lie like barriers in the way of a correct identification and/or evaluation of the usual. When searching for the usual amidst a mass of data you may all too readily be deceived by

1. what seems usual, but isn't,
2. what seems unusual, but isn't,
3. what is the same in kind or quality, but differs in quantity, and
4. what is of the same quantity, but differs in kind or quality.

Let's consider each of these deceptive possibilities separately in the order listed.

1. *What Seems Usual, but Isn't*

"This will be a piece of cake; it's just like the case I wrapped up successfully last week." Rarely is this so. Usually one deceives himself when he arrives at that conclusion.

The danger in such thinking is the danger of superficiality. When a counselor is convinced, on the basis of surface factors, that he is dealing with a Xerox copy of another case, he will be tempted to do an inadequate job of data gathering. I have already mentioned this problem and in the previous chapter urged thoroughness and tentativeness while one awaits sufficient and convincing evidence.

Two wives ordered their husbands out of the house. Does that mean the two cases are alike? No. They are not, as we shall see, except in that one fact alone. Think of some of the many variables in the two cases. (I can't begin to mention them all.) One husband egged his wife on to do so, while the other begged his wife to let him stay: egging and begging are opposites in this instance. In the one case the occasion for the wife's action was the revelation of an extramarital affair; in the other, it was an argument over disciplining the children. One wife is sorry for her words and actions; the other insists that she was entirely justified in what she did. One husband is glad to be out from under the roof, but the wife is sorry that he went. The other husband is sorry, and she is glad. And . . . so it goes. Two cases hardly could be less alike.

The only safe rule is to strip off the wrapper (or wrappers; sometimes a case is multi-wrapped and packaged) and look at what is inside *in every case*. People are not like sticks of chewing gum, where you can be reasonably sure that one is like another by looking at wrappers alone. If you do not make it a rule to examine *every* case, in all details, as thoroughly as you can, you will soon find that instances of insight will grow fewer and fewer and that your ability to pick out common threads diminishes. If this superficiality persists, you soon may begin to lose confidence in your ability to counsel.

I have mentioned this because it is usual for counselors who have progressed to the place where they are beginning to achieve a number of successes in counseling to be tempted to take shortcuts. If you are helping people, the word gets out; more come for help. Your schedule crowds up, and you look for ways to cut down on the time it takes to deal with a person. There will, of course be some acceptable shortcuts that you will learn to use as you grow in experience,[1] but this is not one of them. One reason for the success that the Christian Counseling and Educational Foundation has had is the insistence on thorough data gathering in every case. Taking the time here, in the long run, will save everybody lots of time and plenty of agony. Therefore, make it a rule *never* in *any* counseling case, to fail to take the time to do a full analysis of each case, omitting no avenues that might be explored—especially

---

1. Actually, these are matters of more efficiency.

under the illusion that "this is just like the case I closed out three days ago." Every counselee's life is important enough for you to fully gather all the facts about his problem so that you can give him the best counsel possible. And remember, most important of all is the fact that biblical counseling involves the ministry of God's Word. We dare not take any unwarranted shortcuts in representing Him to men.

2. *What Seems Unusual but Isn't*

The opposite problem, likewise, can occur: factors in a case may look very different from what you usually find and have come to expect in that sort of case, when all the while you have been deceived into thinking them different by their unusual wrappings. Here, the labeling, the situation in which the problem occurs, or other packaging features may deceive. The same candy bar, a British child soon discovers, may have different wrappers; but an American looking for "Turkish Delight" may be deceived by the variety of wrappers in which it is sold.

Often a counselee is the source of the confusion. He may protest, "But, you see, my situation is different." That is what the Corinthians thought, and so Paul had to assure them otherwise:

> No trial has taken hold of you except that which other people have experienced; but God is faithful Who will not allow you to be tried beyond what you are able to bear, but rather, will provide together with the trial the way out so that you may be able to endure it (I Cor. 10:13).

Frequently, when zeroing in on a sin with which a counselee does not want his counselor to meddle, he will protest that "there are differences." And, of course, there always are. So there were for the Corinthians. But it is the counselor's task to determine whether these differences are incidental and peripheral or fundamental and essential. That is to say, he must decide *whether the differences make a difference* in the matter under consideration. Paul had to convince the Corinthians that in their situation they did not. A Christian counselor frequently will have to do the same (on the use of I Cor. 10:13, see my pamphlet, *Christ and Your Problems*).

"But, he did it again—for the fifth time!" Does that make a difference? Must the offended party forgive the repentant offender after five times, just as he would after one offense? Yes. There is no essential difference, our Lord told us in Luke 17:3, 4:

> "Be on your guard. If your brother sins, rebuke him; if he repents, forgive him. And if he sins against you seven times a day and returns to you seven times saying, 'I repent,' forgive him."

As far as *forgiving* is concerned, five times or seven times, or even seventy times, is the same. On that question, the difference makes no difference at all. But if you are discussing the offender's problem and his ability to overcome it, the difference may be quite substantive. A single offense, not repeated, may mean that there was no pattern, while repeated offenses may indicate just the opposite. A counselor will have to handle the two situations quite differently because of the difference between a single act and a pattern.

But, to return to the offended party, he must be told that his protest against the requirement to forgive, even after five offenses, is wrong. The difference makes no difference for him.

3. *What Is the Same in Kind or Quality, but Differs in Quantity*

Size, number, or intensity can make a difference. Consider the following circumstance. When a woman in Tulsa, Oklahoma, slams her car into traffic signs, parked automobiles, and iron fences,[2] after an argument with her boyfriend, in all making a total of 25 hits, the very enormity of the accident has a lot to say about the person in question. If this woman were to seek counsel, the counselor could not avoid taking this factor into consideration. It would not be enough to say, "She has a temper," and leave it at that. Nor would it be adequate to say, "After the quarrel, she had an accident." There is something about the continued, determined effort of the woman driver who, in parking lots, in streets, and on sidewalks, went on and on demolishing everything in her pathway and creating an estimated $20,000 worth of damage, that makes the event special. I think we can all see that.

Now, we must be careful here. The unusual nature of the event must not distract from the fact that there is, beneath it, a routine explanation. Not having had more contact with the case than what I read in the

---

2. *Macon Telegraph*, December 12, 1980.

newspaper, I cannot say what that explanation is. It may be drugs, sleep loss (or some chemical malfunction of the body) that accounts for the intensity of the crime. On the other hand, it may be some pent-up bitterness and anger that at long last was loosed in one grand orgy of destruction never before rivaled by a woman driver. I don't know. But, if I were counseling her, I'd want to know; the intensity of the event must be accounted for, and in that accounting would be the clue to the ordinary and routine. To focus on the event itself, rather than what it points to, however, would be a mistake; it would involve the error of missing the dynamic for its manifestation.

Now, in the case above the importance of intensity, number, quantity, etc., for pointing to the underlying dynamic is obvious. But most of the cases dealt with in the counseling room will not have made the national headlines. And often in these cases, when the data are presented to the counselor, even when in some way or other they may be comparable to this woman driver's bizarre actions, they will be described in words like "after the quarrel, she had an accident." Unless the counselor himself digs out the specific data relating to quantity or intensity, therefore, it turns out that he is dealing with what can only be termed misinformation. To say "she had an accident" simply does not describe *that* event. Quantity of this sort means a change in the quality that cannot be passed over. Oversalting the peas is not the same as salting them. To ignore or tone down the facts means to risk the possibility of failing to grasp their significance—what they say about the true nature of the event and the attitude and behavior of the counselee.

This discussion should point up the fact that the truly unusual may be misidentified as the usual by understatement (or overstatement) of the facts. That, in turn, leads to missing the clue in the unusual character of the event that would point to the usual dynamic beneath.

For some strange reason, there is a class of counselees (and it is not a small number either) who characteristically misstate facts in order to cover over the true nature of the events that happened. I am not speaking of the counselee himself—that is understandable, if not excusable. I'm not even speaking of anyone who has been offended by him. (If it is his spouse, her reluctance to tell the truth can be understood, perhaps as a fear of reprisals. Also, offended persons sometimes withhold truth in order not to look so foolish themselves.) What I have in mind is a misstatement of the facts by interested informants, like family, friends, neighbors presumably trying to help the person who has come for counseling. Perhaps the tendency to downplay the unusual is a gesture of misplaced kindness, but, in the end, it backfires and turns out to be a great unkindness if it throws the counselor off the track of truth.

Of course, the problem can run the other way: "I tell you, he's done it time and time again. Every time I turn around another check has bounced."

"Really? That's a serious problem. How often since you were married 19 years ago has Wallace writtens bad checks?"

"Oh, I don't know; but it seems like we're always getting one back."

"Wallace, Flo says that this happens continually, but she can't give me any specifics. Can you tell me how often continually means?"

"Sure, pastor. Four times in 19 years of marriage. And every time it was because she failed to deposit the check on time."

New counselors would hardly believe that such a conversation could take place, but it does—*routinely!* Because of this, it is important for counselors to check out the facts in detail; they must not settle for generalizations. They must work with specific, concrete (and when important, numerical) details. The interesting thing is that Wallace, like so many others, probably would not have revealed the truth of the situation unless the counselor probed him for it.

There is another related problem. It may occur this way: "First in New York state he spent all his money on drink, moved from job to job, promising to support his wife but didn't. And now, after moving to escape the bill collectors, he has begun to do the same thing all over again in North Carolina. Don't you think he's crazy or something?"

Naturally, this is very hard on his wife and children. But, on the other hand, what is so unusual about it? Isn't that what we'd *expect* of an unbelieving husband, caught in a sinful web of his own weaving, who has no power, direction, purpose, or biblical incentive to extricate himself? Why should we expect the cat to bark?

Just as it is the nature of the cat to meow, not to bark, so it is the nature of the unregenerate person to act in ways like this. In this case, the number of times this husband repeats the pattern only serves to emphasize the fact that it is a pattern. Certainly, it doesn't warrant the conclusion that he is crazy. Here the number of occurrences points to *repetition*, thus marking the behavior itself as a pattern, i.e., as usual, not extraordinary. In the case of the driver, the number of items destroyed in her one-woman demolition derby points to the intensity of the single event rather than to a pattern. In her case, the unusual must be used as an index of some factor unusual for her, which to the counselor is the usual cause of such behavior.

In the woman's case, as I have noted, she may have been drinking, or perceptually affected by drugs, or by sleep loss or body chemistry. On the other hand, there may have been growing manifestations of temper, each more intensive than the former one, leading up to this event. We simply do not know; the newspaper account fails to give us the data. The counselor with a past, however, will not have notes in his file folder that read like the news account; his notes will go far beyond that. He will want to know, and will do everything that is biblically legitimate to discover, just what was going on in the event that led to the series of accidents. Why? Because he is looking for the usual behind the unusual. Only when he finds it will he be able to evaluate the event fully in all of its dimensions in accurate, biblical terms; only then will he be able to help the counselee to do about it what the Bible directs in such a case.

4. *What Is of the Same Quantity, but Differs in Kind or Quality*

You are standing on a street corner. A thoughtless motorist drives rapidly through a nearby mud puddle and splatters you from head to foot. You are upset; quite upset. But wait a minute. Run the scene again. This time as you are standing there, minding your own business, the same motorist approaches slowly and stops. He gets out and comes your way. Suddenly, he reaches down, scoops up a handful of mud and smears it over you from head to foot. This time you are *furious*.

Why the different reactions? In both instances, your clothes are a mess. The amount of mud is approximately the same; the fact is that in quantity and in physical result there is no appreciable difference.

"But," you protest, spitting mud as you speak, "in the first scene the motorist did it thoughtlessly, unintentionally. In the second scene, he did it purposely—with malicious forethought! There is no way that I could have mistaken his intentions; he *wanted* to muddy me up. That's what makes the difference!''

And so it does. When a counselor considers only one aspect of a situation—in this case, the amount of mud and its soiling effects—he may fail to interpret the situation accurately. He may make a situation seem usual in ways that it is not. Here, the emphasis must be on the kind or quality of the event, not merely on the effect or end result.

Intent or attitude or motive is a thorny area where the counselor must tread very carefully, i.e., biblically. It is a difficult area in which to travel. We must be careful not to judge motives; only God can read hearts. But we must read actions (God has called us to do so: ''By their fruit. . . .''), some of which give rather clear indications of intent. But be very cautious; the action must be as clear as the mud-smearing incident. And, of course, we may also ask the counselee questions about his intent and motives and may judge and act on what another says about these matters. But we may *not* try to read another's hidden purposes. God has not given us the right or the ability to do that.

In the mud-smearing incident, the usual factor will not be found by focusing on the results, but on the factor (as yet unknown) that lies beyond—the intent. We do not know why the motorist acted as he did. All we can say for sure is that he intended to do what he did; that we can learn from the action itself. Perhaps he mistook you for another person. Perhaps he was drunk or playing a practical joke, or trying to win a bet. Who knows? The action does not tell us. The usual is not yet available. In counseling we would focus, therefore, not *only* on the action; whatever the motive, it seems wrong in itself (though, possibly, by some weird explanation a good intent could be inferred. More data are necessary).

Now, take another situation. Two men regularly fail to tell their wives that they love them. One fails because of thoughtlessness, embarrassment (some men are brought up with the macho idea that such talk is ''mushy'' and ''unmanly''). The other does not tell her because he hates her. To see in the second situation the same counseling problem as in the first because of the similarities in result could be nothing less than a tragic mistake. To offer as a solution some plan that, in effect, says, ''Each day, tell your wife 'I love you' at breakfast, when you come home, and before you go to sleep at night,'' would be the height of folly.

Yet, there are counselors who do just that sort of thing all of the time.

The usual that a counselor is looking for is not in the common effect on the wives (both may say, ''I am really disappointed that he doesn't say he loves me'') but is in the area of attitude behind each failure. Plainly, as I have presented the cases, there are two dynamics at work, each quite different from the other, and each will require a distinct solution appropriate to it (though this solution will be the one that is usual to the dynamic in each case). Each attitude is representative of very common phenomena with which counselors deal regularly.

So it is as important for a counselor to identify those things which differ as it is to identify those which are similar. Until it is quite clear to him what is unusual and what is usual about a case, he will not have the insight to identify the situation biblically and to propose the biblical solution appropriate to the problem. As you can see from the examples just considered, the usual and the unusual are vital concerns for a biblical counselor. What is usual is the sinful, human dynamic at work. That dynamic can be described in biblical terms; what is unusual will be found in the other features of the case, which may or may not point to the usual but must never be confused or identified with it.

PART TWO

CREATIVITY

7

WHO NEEDS CREATIVITY?

You do. You may dispute the fact. You may even object that "only God creates; I don't have creativity because, not being God, I am therefore totally incapable of it."

Of course only God creates in the absolute sense of the term. That is not in dispute. He alone can bring into being that which previously did not exist. The fact declared in Genesis 1:1 can be attributed to none other than God.

But we must be careful not to be more scrupulous in our use of language than the Scriptures themselves. The Hebrew word *bara*, used in Genesis 1:1 to refer to creation out of nothing, also appears in contexts in which it has a different significance. In addition to carrying the meaning of absolute creation, the word means "to renew" (cf. parallelism in Ps. 51:10; 104:30),[1] "to produce" or "to do something new" (cf. parallelism in Isa. 43:1, 7).[2]

In all of these places the ideas of *newness, productivity,* and *forming* are fundamental.[3] And it is just those ideas that, in part, inhere in the modern English usage of the word "creativity." To speak of a counselor or preacher as creative means that he has the ability to produce new forms, concepts, etc., out of previously existing ones. It means that he is able to shape old things in new ways. Creativity is the art of making old things new. It is producing a thousand songs from eight notes.

I must confess that I am not altogether happy about the use of the English word "creativity" to describe activities attributable to man. My reservation comes from the fact that in addition to the ideas of newness, productivity, and forming, in the biblical use of *bara* there also seems to be a reference, however remote in any given passage, to the power of

---

1. *Bara* is paralleled with *chadash*, "to be new, to renew, to restore."
2. The parallel here is with *yatzar*, "to form, fashion or shape."
3. However, it is true that *bara* is used exclusively of the activities of God.

God. That element, if indeed I am correct in assuming its presence in the word *bara,* of course must be eliminated from any modern use of the term if by it one infers that man has anything like such power *in himself.*[4] And yet, because he has been created in God's image, he does possess certain characteristics that animals do not that may rightly be called creative. Every cat and every dog goes through the same basic routines that cats and dogs have followed for centuries. Circumstances regulate minor differences in detail for them, but there is no growth, no development, no improvement on the part of animals; they simply are not creative.

Man, however, is quite different. He devises tools and appliances, invents new ways of doing old things, alters routines, abandons past ideas and practices in favor of new ones, builds on the past, and so forth. Man is constantly forming new ideas and producing new things. He has a great capacity for newness. Indeed, man can even undergo the utter transformation called the new birth. Though he is passive in that transformation (no dead person could give life to himself), nevertheless, it demonstrates that there is a human potential for radical change. Animals cannot experience regeneration and conversion. The fact that regeneration in no way alters man's humanness so that he is rendered something other than human by it plainly shows that man, *as man,* has a large potential for change.

These new things are new because they did not exist before, even though the ideas and the materials from which they come did. New things are the product of new thoughts, as I have just inferred. An automatic washing machine is a new thing in the history of the world. But first it was a new thought, foreign, for example, to Julius Caesar. Oh, he might have said (in Latin, of course), "Wouldn't it be great to have some way of washing clothes other than by hand," but he never conceived of the contraption that you and I are privileged to use every day. He could not because he never dreamed of electricity or about the millions of uses and adaptations to which it may be put. Indeed, we ourselves have little idea of what man will be doing with electricity, or some other yet undiscovered force, even 50 years from now. All this,

---

4. Any limited, creative powers man possesses must be attributed to the grace of God.

and much, much more has resulted from a God-given ability in man to conceive of and to produce new things that are adaptations of old ones. The new (e.g., washing machines) is built on the older discoveries (e.g., electricity), and so progress occurs. That ability to produce and form new ideas, and those things which flow from these ideas, as a dim reflection of the absolute creative ability of God, not too unfairly we call creativity. So, as I use the word, I am thinking of this—a human creativity, derived, limited, and wholly dependent. The fact must be kept in view as you read this book.

I will use the word, reluctantly (I still wish there were another term), because (1) it is a fairly accurate description of what I shall be discussing, and (2) I know of no other English word that as closely captures the essential factors at work in the conceptualizing and subduing activities of man. Creativity is what is involved in arranging, shaping, and adapting the elements of the original creation that God gave us and told us to bring under control. That is the meaning of the command in Genesis 1:28. Man was commanded to bring the world completely under God's power by discovering the ways and means that He provided.[5]

Biblical creativity requires the use of the imagination within the framework of, and according to, biblical principle. Creative imagination puts to work such capabilities as insight, adaptation, synthesis, and analysis. Each of these is important in its own right, but in this book I must focus attention on insight in its interplay with creativity in counseling. My concern with these two factors will, I hope, bring about an interfacing of the usual with the unique.

Productive counseling, for instance, requires the ability to use biblical principles (the usual) to meet the particular problems (the usual) that a counselee (the unique) is facing in his situation (the unique). That means that the usual and the unique must be brought together in a fruitful manner. To do so, the principle must be applied and implemented by the development of practical how-to in such a way that it fits exactly the problems under consideration. To do so requires creative imagination. This must be used at two points:

---

5. This is the command to be creative. If someone still objects to the word, let him speak of *subduing*.

1. In application of biblical principles;
2. In implementation of biblical principles.

You may have wondered by now why I am discussing creativity in the same book in which I discuss insight. The answer is that the two are related to one another as two contrasting or approximating parts of a whole. Let me briefly contrast the two, show how they complement one another in the work of counseling, and how they describe two essential sides of the counseling process. Each is incomplete without the other.

If we have learned by now that insight is not a mysterious ability akin to a sixth sense, tea reading, or palmistry, as some seem to think, but that it is a matter of knowing accurately and broadly the ordinary problems in which sinners manage to entangle themselves, and the principal biblical precepts that must be used to analyze each problem correctly, together with those that point the way out of the problem,[6] what I have said, in effect, is that insight deals with the *usual*.

Now, in contrast, we may say that creativity is concerned about the *unique*. By that I refer to those elements of a counseling case that make it different from any other (even if in its superficial aspects) and that therefore require unique applications and/or implementations of the usual, ordinary biblical solutions to the common problems that are encountered. Whereas the task in developing insight is to acquire the skills for discovering as many of the ordinary elements in a counseling situation as bear directly or indirectly on the case, in contrast, the task in acquiring the skills of creativity is to learn how to particularize the ordinary biblical solutions so that, without distorting the same, these principles may be exactly fitted to the problem.

After the usual has been isolated and identified as such, it is the special province of creativity to deal with whatever remains that bears upon the matter of application or implementation. Such questions as "What does this principle mean in Fred's case? How can he apply it where he now is? What would be the first thing for him to do?," usually will require creative answers.

---

6. I have not said anything in detail about this aspect of insight in this book simply because all of the rest of my books on counseling have presented precisely that. They are treatises on what is wrong with counselees, biblically speaking, and what the Bible says to do to right these wrongs. The focus in this book is different.

To develop it more clearly, let's consider Fred's problem concretely. It is a problem of responsibility. There's nothing unusual or unique about that. But consider this: Fred has been a youth worker in a church in which he spent most of his time pursuing a girl rather than working with the young people. He was a success in his matrimonial pursuits but a dismal failure as a youth worker. The second year he was not asked to return. He had failed to assume his obligations and to take his responsibilities seriously. He is now married. As he and his wife reflect on the time he spent at the church as a youth worker, Fred becomes convicted of his sin and wonders what he must do to right the wrongs that now seem so obvious and so heinous to him, but which at the time he justified by such rationalizations as "they're not paying me for any more work than they're getting."

As a counselor, you are able to help Fred identify a number of biblical principles that pertain to his case. Fred has been stealing, has been holding bitterness within, has been unfaithful to his obligations before man and God, was more interested in selfish pursuits than in his God-given ministry. All of these patterns, and perhaps others, give biblical insight into what Fred's problem is. They are ordinary, common problems found frequently among sinners and elicit no surprises. However, you may never have dealt with a case exactly like this one before. Having laid these usual features of the case aside, several items remain that have something to do with the case. They are its unique features, and they demand a creative response. Here are two:

1. Fred now lives 1,000 miles away from the church that he cheated.
2. Fred is, himself, now the pastor of a small congregation.

Fred is now repentant, and you have had no difficulty in persuading him that he should seek God's forgiveness for his sins. The question that the two of you are struggling with is how Fred may best confess his sin to the congregation and how he may offer to make restitution?

Does he write, phone, or attempt to make a personal visit? To whom does he address the call or the letter if that proves the best way to make contact? To the pastor? To the chairman of the board that hired him? To the young people? To their parents? To all, or to some of the above?

Moreover, he wants to know about restitution. If the congregation does not refuse to accept an offer of restitution, what may he offer to do, given the distance and his limited finances? And what about his new responsibilities? Surely, he must not sacrifice them for older ones.

Here is where a creative application and implementation of biblical principles will be necessary. There is no biblical passage addressed directly to delinquent youth workers who live 1,000 miles from those they have offended. Passages about forgiveness, reconciliation, and restitution must be applied creatively. The basic dynamics are ordinary; the particular features of the case are not. And the chances are that Fred will be perplexed about what steps to take and will ask for advice from the counselor.

It will not be enough for Fred's counselor to say, "Confess your sins and make restitution" and leave it at that. That is why so much counseling fails. If you do that, Fred may simply give up, do the wrong thing, or continue to worry about the problem. The counselor may ask Fred for suggestions, may point to possible ideas that occur to him, and may interact with Fred as together they consider various alternatives and their possible consequences, but they must have developed a concrete plan of action to which Fred is committed before that counseling task is completed. Like John the Baptist, who called men to repentance, the counselor must be ready and able to tell those who ask, something that fits each unique situation (note in Luke 3:10-14 how he gave each repentant class advice that creatively fits it).

The facts are clear enough; insight uncovers and analyzes these. The general situation is equally clear. But the specific acts, how to perform them, when and where, all must be developed by creative application of biblical principles.

The case just mentioned poses the problems. The creative responses needed in the case have been omitted purposely in order to (1) get the reader to think creatively about a concrete case and (2) provide a case to test against the ideas and explanations that are given in the succeeding chapters. In order to test your present creative capabilities, list in the space below five suggestions regarding this case that come to mind.[7] (Reconsider your suggestions later in the light of what you have studied.)

---

7. Take about as much time as a counselor would have to think in a counseling session.

List your suggestions in the left hand column. After finishing the book, return to this page, consider your suggestions, and make any revisions or comments you think are appropriate.

SUGGESTIONS	COMMENTS
1.	
2.	
3.	
4.	
5.	

8

I DON'T HAVE WHAT IT TAKES

"O.K., so maybe I need creativity for counseling. But I question one thing you've said; you've been talking like creativity is an ability that almost anyone can develop. I really doubt that. You are going to have to do some convincing before I'll accept it. I still think it is something some people are born with, and not others. It's true that I thought the same about insight, and I agree that you've pretty well taken the mystery out of that one, but creativity is different, isn't it? I don't see how a person can *learn* a thing like that. As I now look at myself, I'd say that there is little, if anything, about me that is creative; if you can teach me creativity, you can teach anybody. But, I don't think you can. Creativity is like artistic and musical ability, isn't it? Either you have it or you don't. And I just don't have what it takes."

Your questions are understandable, and it takes a little insight to recognize them as arising from the unbiblical philosophies in which we all have been marinated for so long. But I won't go into that.

There are just two replies that I wish to make at this point. To all that I have to say here about creativity (the art of conceptualizing and producing the new or unusual), what it consists of and how to learn it, later I shall add a third. But now, consider these two facts:

1. If biblical counseling is required of all Christians (and it is; see *Competent to Counsel, The Christian Counselor's Manual,* and *Ready to Restore*), and if creativity is an essential ingredient in counseling (and you have admitted that it is), then *all* Christians are capable of learning how to be creative. Not all will be *as* creative as others, doubtless, but each may become creative enough to discharge the duties of counseling that God lays upon him. I need say no more about this because, in itself, it should clinch the issue.

2. You are already a creative person, though you are unaware of the fact. This is the point I wish to develop, because I think it will help you to see clearly what I am trying to say. Every day, all day long, you act

creatively in many little ways that your daily activities require of you. Let us take the typical housewife. As she is washing the windows, she runs out of paper towels. Looking around for something that she can use as a substitute to finish the job, she spots a box of facial tissues. She uses these and with little loss of efficiency achieves the same result. That was an instance of creativity.

"Big deal," you sneer. "Anyone reading this book would have done the same."

Big deal, indeed! If you still maintain that you are uncreative, you *should* consider it a big deal. Of course anyone reading this book would have done the same; that's just the point. But nonetheless, it was creativity that led her to substitute tissues for towels. What makes you sneer at my example is the fact that the substitution was so common, so natural, so simple, so easy, so like what we do all the time that one would not ordinarily *call* it creative. In other words, creativity for this housewife simply was *not* a big deal. But that doesn't make it any the less creative. It just shows how creative we all are all of the time. Think of how often we do such things every day. It is questionable whether a person can survive on his own without creativity.

If the housewife had never before substituted tissues for towels to clean window panes, the act was truly creative: she produced what was for her a brand new tool when she put a familiar item to a new and unfamiliar use. In the unique situation (running out of paper towels) she did not do the usual (go buy some more); she innovated to meet her need.

In this example you can see, on a small scale, the origin of the old saying, "Necessity is the mother of invention." If you need something, but do not have the usual tool to produce it, you must invent, substitute, or adapt something for the purpose at hand. That is creativity at work. Creativity in counseling is not unlike it. Let us consider a simple case.

Bob, a conscientious pastor, has been foolishly accepting too many nighttime appointments. He finds himself out nearly every evening. He is convicted that to be absent from his wife and children that often is sin. Church work has been taking priority over family. In discussion with another pastor, they find that he has a hard time in saying no. Together they examine the problem. There seems to be a pattern: When asked to take on a responsibility, he becomes enthusiastic, wants to help out, and on the spot whips out his appointment book and writes in another engagement. Then, when he gets home, calms down, reflects on the inadvisability of what he has done, prays, and talks it over with his wife, all too often he regrets his previous hasty action. "If only I hadn't acted so quickly on emotion," he catches himself saying again and again.

Now, given this pattern and his desire to discontinue the sin involved, what will he do to guard against the problem in the future? He wants to please God by putting his family before his work. (He recognizes that it is also the Lord's work to be a proper husband and father and a good example of both to the flock.) That is not the problem. What Bob and his counselor need to work on is the implementation of this good resolution. If he is told, "Stop doing it," or "Do what you know the Lord wants you to do," or other pious platitudes of the sort, it will not help him overcome the habit pattern that he wants to put off. There must be a way of

1. reminding him of his commitment in times of temptation,
2. overcoming the emotion of the moment,
3. making it easier to say no,
4. giving more mature, prayerful thought to such decisions, and
5. making it hard to say yes on the spot.[1]

When they analyze the problem this way (notice creativity grows out of a careful analysis[2] of the problem), several elements in the analysis point to the solution that they reached. What follows is sort of a digest of the thinking and the reasoning that went on as the two men grappled with the problem. The counselor is speaking:

"1. Something in the situation must be changed (creativity) to remind you every time, without fail, of your new commitment. You are the only constant factor; so it must be a change in your usual pattern of action.

"2. But, because you tend to get into trouble when you are in emotionally charged situations where you let your enthusiasm run away with you, the change must involve an automatic process; otherwise, we cannot depend on you to produce each time.

---

1. See the section on radical amputation in my book, *More than Redemption*, for the dynamic behind several of these requirements. Jesus had very strong admonitions to make about prevention of problems in the future. In the example with which we are now working, the cutting off of the right hand is best implemented by ridding himself of the appointment book, as we shall see.

2. Analysis means breaking a problem into its constituent parts. See the next chapter.

"3. It must be a change that makes it hard for you to say yes and easier for you to say no.

"4. And, the change must allow you time to talk, think, and pray in a calmer atmosphere about each potential engagement before reaching a decision."

As the problem was broken down this way, the two thought about the various elements in the situation and concluded that there was only one factor to which all of these requirements pointed: the appointment book. Listen, again, to the counselor:

"You look at it each time—if you wrote a reminder on each page, that might help. . . . No, that's not automatic enough. You might fail to do so, or you could ignore it out of the enthusiasm of the moment. The *every time without fail* factor is not satisfied.

"Hmmmmmm . . . let's see. The change must make it possible to prolong the decision and must make it hard to say yes, while at the same time making it easy to say no. Mmmmmmmmmm. . . . Let's see. . . .

"I've got it! You stop carrying an appointment book. Yeah . . . that would do it! You won't say yes because you won't dare do so—you may already have another engagement for that hour. But without your book, you won't know. And . . . you will be reminded *every* time of your commitment when you reach into your pocket and find that the book is missing. That will give you time to think, talk to your wife and pray before making decisions. And you will be able to do so in a calmer atmosphere when the emotion has subsided, because you will have to wait until you go home and look at your book to decide. And it will work every *time*. . . . Or will it?

"No . . . wait a minute . . . There's a hitch: suppose out of habit or in a weak moment you take your appointment book anyway. . . . We'll have to overcome that hazard. . . ."

"I know," says Bob, "I'll throw the old one away and buy an appointment calendar that's too large to put into my pocket. That ought to do it."

"Right! That's a great idea. And make it large enough not to fit into your briefcase. Remember those committee meetings!"

There, in a very simple matter, you see the process of creativity at work. Surely, *that* is not beyond you. Will Bob need to follow this course indefinitely? Perhaps. Probably, however, after some time he will begin to master the problem and may begin to sneak a medium-sized appointment book into his briefcase when, beforehand, during cool deliberation, he decides that he will need it for a particular purpose. He might be wise never to carry a small calendar again. It is so easy to avoid commitments by saying, "I'm afraid I can't give you an immediate answer; I don't have my appointment book. Will you please call me tomorrow?"

Now, let's look at the counseling example that we have just concluded. What makes the solution creative?

What makes Bob's decision creative is the fact that he had never done it (or even thought of it) before. It was *new* to him. It is a new use of old ideas to meet a particular situation. It meets old needs in new ways.

For the counselor it is creative because he had never had to face exactly this situation before, so that he had never suggested anything exactly like it before. The basic problem was responsibility to family and the setting of priorities; that was the common insight problem that for the creative solution was laid aside. The new way of handling it was stimulated by the process of analysis in which the counselor engaged, and into which Bob entered enthusiastically, even to suggest and clinch the final form in which the solution was cast. This process broke down the problem into its several aspects, each of which had to be considered in the final solution. These aspects of the problem he considered conditions to be met. Thus they became criteria by which to judge the worth of any solutions that might be proposed.

The creative ability of others often emerges as they are brought into the creative process. We saw how Bob joined in. It is wise, therefore, for those counselors who have the opportunity to meet together with other counselors of like mind, to go over cases together, using the *Christian Counselor's Casebook* or personal cases that they themselves have been engaged in. (The problem with using one's own cases is that often one is tempted to waste time getting off into esoteric details or other types of sidelines. And, it is easy to develop blind spots to facts.) Together, they may work on case after case, trying to come up with joint solutions that creatively meet the situations posed by the problems encountered.

If Bob's counselor, or Bob himself, for that matter, uses the same idea again with another counselee who has the same problem, the solution will no longer require creativity. It will have become usual, a part of his counseling repertoire, a stock, routine response. But, it is possible (perhaps more likely than not) that the next case, involving a business-man, let us say, will be different enough in detail to require some variation on this theme.

The solution, once reached, is capable of countless adaptations that a creative counselor, called upon to meet the needs of counselees in a wide variety of circumstances, will find himself exploring. Creativity in these subsequent cases will be stimulated by success in the original case, by the direction that the basic solution provides, etc. The counselor who fails to grow in creativity will freeze-dry this solution and refuse to modify or adapt it. The danger is that he may become satisfied and hesitate to use creativity in this area again out of fear that any adaptation may not measure up to the original one. Or, if he has a tendency toward laziness, he may rigidly cling to the original success as the answer into which all counselees must fit themselves. Failure of creativity can itself, thereby, stem from success in creativity. The "Let's leave well enough alone" attitude, when not really justified, can be deadly to creativity.

On the other hand, success in creativity can lead to an unhealthy interest in creativity itself, focusing on the process rather than on the results, interested in being creative rather than in helping the counselee. When one begins to find creative solutions so much fun to develop, as indeed he will once he begins to become adept at reaching them, he runs the danger of making the creative process a game that he plays with himself and others. It becomes a sort of "Can you top this" challenge instead of a power that one is developing, perfecting, and using to Christ's honor and for the benefit of His flock. Both dangers must be avoided.

Perhaps the very best way to remember the importance of creativity in the work of ministry as well as at the same time reminding one's self of the purpose for which it is to be used is to recall (or even to post in the counseling room at a place conspicuous to the counselor) Jesus' words on creative ministry:

So He said to them, "Therefore, every scribe discipled for the empire from the heavens is like a householder who brings out of his treasure new things and old things'' (Matt. 13:52).

When counseling, the scribe in Christ's kingdom (notice the purpose for which creative ability should be used—for the sake of God's church) truly must bring out of his storehouse things both old and new.[3] The old must not be discarded merely for the sake of novelty, nor must the new be avoided out of fear or lethargy. Both old and new are necessary; biblical ministry involves both the usual and the unique.

In closing, it is worth noting that a counselor with a growing repertory of basic creative solutions finds it easier and easier to adapt and implement biblical principles by making minor creative adjustments to old (now routine) solutions and by combining elements of any two or more.

Perhaps, from the discussion in this chapter, you have now begun to admit, however reluctantly, that it is possible even for you to learn something of the principles and the practice of creativity. If so, let me follow up on that in the chapters that remain, to make the whole matter clearer and easier. You may not yet recognize that you "have what it takes" to be creative, but I hope that at least you suspect that you might. Perhaps what comes next will push you still further along the road toward that conviction.

---

3. Calvin has some interesting remarks on this passage. He says, "Teachers in the church ought to be prepared by long study for giving to the people, as out of a storehouse, a variety of instruction . . . wisely and properly adapted to the capacity of every individual." Calvin believed in a creatively adapted ministry of the Word.

9

ANALYSIS AND SYNTHESIS

In the case discussed in the previous chapter, we saw something of the process of analysis (taking things apart and considering each part separately) and how it provided the way for creativity by showing all the aspects of a solution that needed to be considered. We saw also that proper use of analysis can provide the criteria for determining whether a proposed solution has met the requirements of each aspect of the problem. Now, we want to see synthesis (bringing seemingly unrelated parts together to form a whole) at work in creativity. Synthesis is the opposite of analysis, just as insight is the opposite of creativity (the usual and the unique) but works together with it as parts of a whole. We have seen that creativity involves the substitution of one thing for another, the alteration of something that exists, the combining of various elements, or in some way or another bringing new ideas, new processes, and new items into existence. These *new* factors, in every instance, are built on and formed out of previously existing ones.

In the following example notice how the counselor synthetically brings several isolated, but usual, elements together to form a solution to a problem. The new thing that is produced is the result of this synthesis.

Phil and Marge have been on the brink of divorce. The divorce was averted only by early counseling in which their pastor took the initiative. Love, as giving rather than as feeling, has been thoroughly explained; the husband's biblical role and responsibility both for initiating and for maintaining love in the marriage has been made clear; the duty of living with Marge in an understanding way (I Pet. 3:7) has been enjoined; and Phil, now repentant over his past failures, wants to know how he can learn to love Marge by giving. In commenting on the passage in Peter he muses, "I'm not sure I understand much of anything about her interests, desires, concerns, or whatever. I don't even understand her well enough to know what would please her if I tried to give her something."

Unconscious of the fact, Phil has already begun to engage in the

67

process of creativity. He has *related* (a synthetic action) understanding and giving (something that he has never done before)—but in a negative way. For the first time, he sees that unless he *understands* Marge better he will not be able to *give* her what she needs or wants. The competent counselor would pick up on this and pull the two together into one concrete homework assignment that is designed to solve both problems. It would be an assignment that helps him to learn both how to give and how to understand. He might even stress the fact that the two work together to strengthen each other:

> By giving in the way I suggest, you will come to understand Marge better, which, in turn, will make your giving more intelligent, and you will find yourself hitting the bull's-eye more frequently. You will be living according to knowledge rather than according to ignorance. Now, let me suggest how you can accomplish this. . . .

The counselor then proceeds to describe a plan that will bring these two seemingly discrete, but vitally related factors, giving and understanding, into conjunction:

> For three weeks do one *small* thing for your wife every day simply in an attempt to please her. Marge, you must give Phil honest feedback on whether or not he rings the bell. Phil, this will do two things at once: (1) You will be giving of yourself—your thought, your time, your interest—every day as you do so. That means that you will be beginning to *show* love, even if in very small ways, *every day.* And you will increase your investment in Marge. (2) At the same time, you will be learning what, in fact, does and does not please her. Remember, now, I said one *small* thing. I stress the word small because, as you know, you have little understanding of Marge at present. When you become more proficient at understanding what pleases her, then you can get into bigger things. But don't be surprised if small changes in your behavior may bring about big changes in the relationship.

Now let us ask, just how was the counselor able to give Phil this advice? And, how could he help him to lay out a plan that would implement the biblical principles and practices that were commanded in Ephesians 5:25 and I Peter 3:7?

The answer is by *combining* things that fit together into a new, working synthesis. By analysis, as he discussed Phil's problem, the pastor discovered that Phil did not know that love begins with giving[1] and that he must understand his wife in order to live with her as a Christian husband should. As these problems emerged, actually, it was Phil himself who pointed the way to the creative application of the passages just mentioned. His objection in effect was, "I don't *understand* her well enough to know what to *give* her." Picking up on that, the pastor developed an assignment that led to implementation that *combined* the biblical answer to both problems. Having discovered the two elements by analysis, it was then possible to rearrange the elements into a new constructive biblical synthesis and to move ahead.

Because the pastor believed that God is the God of order and unity, he sought to find a way that both biblical needs could be met in tandem. He knew that obedience to one biblical injunction would strengthen Phil's ability to obey the other one ("The way of Jehovah is strength to the upright," Prov. 10:29) and so sought a way to combine two solutions to each so that they would strengthen each other. The assignment that he devised seemed naturally to grow out of the facts at hand.[2]

Let's look at another instance of synthesis of an altogether different sort. Beth's problem, she says, is that she has forgiven but "cannot forget" the adulterous relationship in which Tom, her husband, had been involved. The illicit affair itself is over and done with; confession and repentance were made and accepted and forgiveness was granted fully five years ago. Both Tom and Beth agree that the repentance was genuine and that ever since Tom has proved to be a good and faithful husband. But during the entire five year period hardly a week has passed in which Tom has not come home from work to find Beth sitting in the sewing room, red-eyed and tearful, sometimes sobbing her heart out. Always, the same explanation is given: "I just can't keep from thinking about you in her arms." How does a counselor deal with this?

Synthetic creativity will be needed to pull together a number of things into one picture because, at the moment, much is missing. What is

---

1. See my book, *The Language of Counseling,* for fuller discussion of this point.

2. Any number of other biblically legitimate combinations were possible. This was not the only way to go; but it was *one* way. I have not gone through all the steps in reaching each feature in the assignment, as I did in the previous chapter when discussing analysis. Here, I have just provided the finished product.

needed is a wholistic, systematic approach to the problem. First, Beth must be taught that *forgiveness is the way of forgetting*. God doesn't say "forgive and forget." (That old saw, like many others similar to it, has done much damage; the harm in it is that it separates the two as though one could actually forgive without forgetting.) The Bible commands, "forgive." Why doesn't it also command us to forget? Because forgiveness, when genuine, always involves forgetting.

Like so many other Christians, Beth was never taught what forgiveness is, and so she does not understand it. When she "forgave" Tom, therefore, she thought that she knew what she was doing, but she really didn't. To say "I forgive you" is to *make a promise*. Beth did not understand this. God's forgiveness of us in Christ is the model for our forgiveness (Eph. 4:32). But what promise does God make when He forgives us? He says, "Your sins and your iniquities will I remember against you no more" (Jer. 31:34). This is a promise to actively remember "no more."[3] Whether we remember one's sins against him or not, therefore, is actually under our control. Forgiving and forgetting are bound up in one another. Because that is so, Beth's problem isn't merely a problem of forgetting but a problem of forgiving. She must first see the two inextricably tied to one another—so closely that she must be brought to realize that she has never really forgiven her husband. That is the basic problem. And to forgive, as we shall see, she must (actively) not remember.

It is true that Beth said, "I forgive you," and according to her inadequate understanding of forgiveness she may genuinely have meant to forgive him. She may have wanted to bury the past and start fresh again; but she didn't. That was because she did not understand forgiveness. When she said "I forgive you," she thought that forgiveness was over and done with. But she was wrong. That isn't all that there is to forgiveness. Forgiveness is a promise, and a promise not only must be *made,* but must be *kept.* Like many Christians, Beth may have thought forgiveness is a feeling to be expressed or merely a declaration to be made rather than a promise to be kept. While good feelings flow from making and keeping the promise of forgiveness, and while the promise is

3. Not just to "forget," which usually is construed as passive. Forgetting is the result of not remembering.

a declaration to another, it is a declaration with a commitment attached (that is to say, it is a *promise*). The element that was lost in her faulty understanding, and from which Tom and she are suffering, is the important fact that forgiveness is a *promise* to be *made* and to be *kept*.

So, in pulling things together, for Beth and for Tom, three matters have to be synthesized into a systematic approach to forgiveness:

1. Forgiveness is a *promise* (this is demonstrated by a discussion of Jeremiah 31).

2. It is inextricably intertwined with forgetting. Indeed, it is a promise to forget: "I will remember your sins against you no more."

3. It is a promise to keep.

In pulling together these loose ends into a whole, the doctrine of forgiveness begins to take clearer shape.[4] In this form, facts creatively new to Beth and Tom (routine for the counselor with a past who has thought deeply about forgiveness) begin to shape the problem and its solution: Beth has not made the promise in understanding and, as a result, she has not kept it; therefore, she must now do both.

Beth could hardly have been expected to make a promise when she was unaware of the fact that forgiveness involves a promise. Indeed, she did not even intend to make a promise and did not do so—it turns out that what she did was merely to express a momentary state of mind and feeling (this has fluctuated since) when she said, "I forgive you," and so she failed to forgive. She has made no effort to remember no more. Instead, she has been remembering for five years!

Therefore, having clarified that point for both Beth and Tom, the counselor will ask Beth to truly forgive Tom at last, promising him this time that she will do whatever God requires to (actively) remember his sin against her no more.

Beth replies, "I'll make the promise because I want to put the whole matter into the past once and for all, but I don't know whether I can keep it. That seems to have been my problem all along. You'll have to help me."

"No, Beth, that hasn't been your problem," replies the counselor.

---

4. For a much more detailed discussion of forgiveness in counseling, see my book, *More than Redemption: A Theology of Christian Counseling*, chapter 13.

"First, because you didn't know that forgiveness is a promise to keep, you were unprepared to keep it. There is a great difference between thinking, 'all I have to do is make a declaration, or express my feeling,' and knowing that you have committed yourself to a course of life for the future. The way you enter into the period that follows each is altogether different. On the first basis all is behind you; nothing more must be done. On the second, the granting of the promise and reconciliation are behind, but the keeping of the promise and the development of a new relationship still lie ahead." Beth had been involved in putting off to some extent, but she had not realized the need for putting on.[5] No wonder she failed; the next five years were programmed for failure.

But there are other factors that also must be pulled together to complete the picture:

1. Beth must understand the full meaning of her promise.
2. She must creatively develop ways to keep the promise.
3. Since for the last five years she has developed patterns for violating her promise, she must learn how to use radical amputation[6] to block and overcome patterns established during that period of time, and she must develop new ways of controlling her thinking.[7]

Unless Beth adopts the think-list approach, or some other creative adaptation of biblical principles to her situation, her hopes of overcoming the problem will be slim. Beth's plea for help is important; a counselor must not ignore such pleas or give pious advice and exhorta-

---

5. See information on the biblical put off/put on dynamic in *The Manual*, chapters 18, 19. See also *Matters of Concern to Christian Counselors*, pp. 36, 37. I say "to some extent" because it is never possible to put off a practice unless at the same time one puts on the biblical alternative. Until the former practice is *replaced* by the new biblical one, it will not be put off. What I should have said, perhaps, is that Beth was involved in *trying* to put off the old ways.

6. See *More than Redemption* for information on this biblical concept.

7. Using perhaps a Philippians 4:8 think-list adapted to her attitudes. She, they, or the counselor may develop another approach that may better fit their situation. This is simply a list of mind-engaging items to think about whenever one catches his thoughts beginning to drift into forbidden territory. It should consist of items that fit the criteria in Philippians 4:8, and should be carried at all times. The counselor in giving the assignment to develop the list may say, "I'll give you the first item as a freebee. Write this under number one: 'Things to put on my Phil. 4:8 think list'; that should get you the rest."

tion in response. Unless the counselor helps her concretely, creatively, she will be at sea.

It should be clear from this discussion that successful counseling requires synthetic work. Counselors may not simply exhort and hand out Bible verses. They must *minister* the Word. Ministering the Word requires application and help with implementation as well. Verses must be explained and related to the particular circumstances at hand. All this must be done systematically and practically. The counselor cannot leave matters dangling; he must be sure that counseling not only wraps up the problem but puts a ribbon on it with the bow tied tightly. Any lesser use of the Scriptures may lead to defeat and discouragement and, as the upshot of that, to a weakening of faith in God's faithfulness and in the power of His Word.

10

HINDRANCES TO CREATIVITY

Doubtless, there are dozens of factors that could be mentioned when considering possible hindrances to creativity, but I wish to discuss only two: fear and lack of method. The two are not mutually exclusive.

If one is stuck in his routines, comfortably doing things the way he always has, you can almost always count on the fact that he fears change. He may fear it because of a fear of the unknown or because of laziness. (Upsetting one's routine and learning new things require work, which he fears.) Budging persons who are satisfied with the status quo, therefore, is not easy. It is altogether possible that some of those who object to creativity, supposedly on intellectual grounds, and some of those who protest that they could never become creative are, in reality, acting out of fear.

Change (and the new or unique always requires some change) inevitably disturbs the status quo. And, although one's counseling routine may not be very effective, at least it is predictable, and to that extent, safe! Who knows where change would take him and through what new labyrinths he may have to wander if he opts for the creative approach? "No," he thinks, "let the counselee adapt to *me* and the way *I* do things; that's better than adapting to his circumstances;[1] who knows what sorts of problems that might get me into?"

Though underneath he is dissatisfied with the present way of doing things, he is afraid of change and the unknown: "the status quo may not be all that good, but something else may be far worse," he tells himself. And, at length, he may even begin to convince himself that his present methods are rather good after all.

Of course, as I have pointed out, this sort of thinking is based on selfish motives. Counselors who think of their own comfort, who will not take risks (of failure, embarrassment, etc.) really do not care enough

---

1. Actually, there should be mutual adaptation. Both must be willing to change.

for their counselees or for God to do the hard work of *growing*. Growth. always means abandoning old ways (cf. I Cor. 13:11) in favor of new ones. The fear of newness, in the final analysis, is always an admission of the lack of love. It is love from God and for Him and one's neighbor that alone has the power to dispel fear (I John 4:18). Love triumphs over fear when one loves enough to risk his own welfare in some way. Maintenance of the status quo, the greatest enemy of creativity, is so often a form of selfishness in which all the risks must be taken by the counselee, while the counselor plays it safe.

But how do Christians get stuck in the status quo? Many influences have a way of bringing this about—pressures from without and from within. Ultimately, the problem is a matter of sin. It is easy to follow the inclination of sinful nature and to adopt and cling to the ways that are immediately comfortable to us. Personal risk and real effort are always avoided by those who seek the easy, comfortable, safe way. Of course, as I noted, this is only *immediately* comfortable. In the long run, following the status quo, with its lack of growth and the insular pursuit of personal interests, rather than the outreaching and expanding risks of love, is self-defeating and destructive and leads to misery. Whoever wants to save his life will lose it; whoever loses it for Christ will save it in the long run.

Yet, there is another reason, or perhaps it would be better to say excuse, that is often seized upon for following the insular rather than the more expansive road of love: the lack of a method for developing creativity. I call this an excuse, even though at first sight it might seem as close to a reason as one might come. The reason for my conclusion is this: if a counselor strongly enough wants to improve on his failures, if he cares enough, if he loves God enough, he will seek until he finds. We would, at the very least, find him out searching; he would be uneasy, dissatisfied; he would never be found stuck in the status quo. And (please don't miss this point) that seeking process, pursued diligently, would have been the first step in developing his creative ability. He would have had to think creatively about the problem. He would have had to find creative (that is, new to him, and perhaps to others) ways of becoming more creative in counseling (or, at the very least, he would have *attempted* them). What I am trying to say is that the diligent, prayerful pursuit of method would itself in time lead to the discovery, development, and deployment of methods. In the end, therefore, what one must conclude is that nearly always Christians are stuck in the status quo because they are unwilling to do anything about it; which in turn means that they lack an impelling desire to please God. No counselor may counsel in that frame of mind. He must repent and get to work.

But I also recognize that the matter isn't always so clearly that simple; the dynamic involved can be quite deceptive. "I'll never be creative; why should I try? It takes a *creative* person to devise ways to be creative." So one may protest. We have seen, however, that like the housewife who substituted tissues for towels, all have the ability to be creative. And all Christians, using the Bible, may do creative things for God. It is precisely in order to obviate and to dispose of this excuse, therefore, that I have entered into this discussion of *ways of stimulating* creativity. After all, when God required us to *give thought*[2] about ways to "stimulate one another to love and fine deeds" (Heb. 10:24), He called us to the work of creative counseling. Christian counselors, in formal and informal settings, have as the goal of their task exactly what the writer of Hebrews urges. We are to creatively help others to creatively observe God's commandments.

And note too that the writer does not merely speak of "love and *good* deeds," as some translations have it, but "love and *fine* deeds." The word used in the Greek (*kalos*) refers not only to the result or the end of the action, but also to the *manner* in which that end is attained: *both* must be "fine." God doesn't care only about ends; He cares also about how they are reached. He wants us both to accomplish His fine will and, while doing so, to do it finely; i.e., with finesse.[3] But finesse calls for creativity. By definition, it goes beyond the ordinary, the routine, the monotonous, the rough, the crude, and the thoughtless. When a woman serves a meal with finesse, she adds all of the extra touches. But that takes time, planning, thought, and extra effort. And it will usually mean

---

2. The word means, literally, "to get your mind down to" the task. The term is a strong one, indicating effort. That means expending thoughtful effort in the pursuit of these ways; God didn't tell us *how* to do this. Instead, He commanded us to use the minds He gave us to think of ways to stimulate others to love and to fine deeds. That command is a call to creativity.

3. For more on this concern for finesse, see chapter 13 of *How to Overcome Evil*.

taking the risk of doing some things that are new to her, like following a new recipe.

Creativity is like that. Through preaching, writing, or counseling one can present God's truth in such a dull, trite, and uninviting way that, in fact, the end product is no longer God's truth. The form in which it has been conveyed has so distorted the truth that it no longer faithfully represents what God has said. God's truth is not dull, trite, and uninviting, but just the opposite. Not only does the end not justify the means, but the means always contributes something to the the end, enhancing or distorting it. Creativity requires time, planning, effort, and thought (as the verse in Hebrews makes plain). To creatively adapt the exciting, inviting, unique truth of God to a modern context, *without accommodation,* cannot be done with less effort or determination.

Accommodation can follow two paths, either of which is disastrous and leads to a distortion of God's Word. The truth itself may be altered, rather than the form in which it is conveyed, (1) by attempting to make it fit the person to whom it is presented or (2) by making it fit the person who is presenting it. We are all familiar with the first sort of distortion— it occurs when one trims his sails (or rather God's sails), watering down some powerful biblical teaching to gain acceptance. But we are not as familiar with the second (although it occurs every bit as often as the first).

The second is a distortion of truth that happens when it is made to fit the one who is presenting it. Here, I am not referring so much to a willing distortion of truth that the one ministering it might effect because of erroneous beliefs, or in order to justify or tone down the biblical condemnation of some sinful lifestyle. Rather, I refer to the more-often-than-not unintended and possibly unrecognized phenomenon that occurs when dull, uncreative people teach and apply God's truth in a manner that grows out of and fits their own lazy or fearful uncreativeness. In so many instances, as a result, counseling falters for no other reason than the lack of creative adaptation (quite different from accommodation[4]) of truth to life.

---

4. Truth *must* be adapted. That is to say, it must be fitted to the time and circumstances, without distortion. This is accomplished by presenting truth in such a way that what was intended is what is conveyed. Exciting material must be presented in exciting form. Distortion can take place when accommodation or a lack of adaptation occurs.

Therefore, we must "give thought to ways" of *stimulating* others to "give thought to ways" of being creative in showing love through fine deeds. That is precisely what I plan to continue to do in the pages that follow. As a matter of fact, this book was written for that very purpose: to stimulate Christian counselors to exert greater love by doing finer work in their counseling. So get ready now to examine a method for smashing status quo thinking and counseling. Naturally, the method will be of little use unless it is given a fair, prayerful try. I trust that if by now you are convicted of the need to become more creative in your counseling, you will do just that.

11

THE THREE Rs

Since the presence or absence of creativity is what so often makes a significant difference between counselors who, in other respects, may be quite similar, it is important to study creativity as fully as possible. So far, we have discovered that insight is the ability to isolate and identify the commonplace, or usual. In contrast, we have seen that creativity is the ability to give the usual a unique twist, to use it for a unique purpose, to adapt it to a unique set of particulars. In short, *creativity is the art of producing newness by forming new concepts and plans of action.*

And, we have seen, generally, this newness occurs in the process of separating from a confused mass and studying those individual elements that one never considered individually in depth before (analysis). And, we have seen how creativity also moves in the opposite direction, pulling together things that one never related systematically before (synthesis). Thus a unique result is obtained by *combining*.

In this chapter, I shall approach the art of newness from a different angle. Here you will find a formula that may be useful for getting the creative process in gear and backing it out of the garage. It is certainly useful whenever you do not know what to do next. It can be easily remembered as the three-R formula:

Review it.
Reverse it
Revise it.

If you keep in mind these three ideas, and what they mean, you can readily rehearse and follow them at any time. They should prove helpful when you know that creativity is needed and you are momentarily stalled. Just one note: use them in the same order for best results.

Review It

By this I mean *go over the counseling data again.* And, if necessary, again and again. It is easy to miss something that is there or the fact that something *ought* to be there that isn't. Either way, what you are doing is looking for more data, or for a sharpening of your understanding of the existing data. Or, if the data are quite adequate, and your understanding is too, your problem may lie in finding the right application of biblical truth to a uniquely different situation, or in its implementation in that new situation. In such cases, review is also of help in shaping that up. It is the use of review that I wish, therefore, to emphasize first.

When you review, do so in meticulous detail. Ask a counselee for material that he did not give you before: exact numbers, what happened next, responses to responses, etc. Ask, "And then, tell me precisely what you said. . . . Good. But *how* did you say that? In what tone of voice?" etc. As you go along, paying attention to details, here and there new ideas will pop up; sometimes they will protrude from the new data. You will be alerted to indicators and pointers that will direct you to creative solutions. Many of these you would never have dreamed up in any other way. Take, for instance, the following example:

> Howard knows that he must return to his wife and that they must begin to live together again this week for the first time in three months. But neither he nor Marcia wants to upset the reconciliation that has been effected during this first counseling session. The counselor is also concerned about the matter. But time is up and only a few minutes can be spent on creative prevention. Yet the pastor wisely reviews in order to discover the exact nature of the problem so that he can suggest a means of prevention. Notice how the solution emerges from the review itself.

Pastor: "Now, this week, I want the two of you to walk on eggs. We haven't had time to work on the principles of communication that seem to be so badly needed in this marriage. And I haven't had time to explain the biblical way to handle anger either. So be sure that you are extra careful not to upset the good work that God has enabled you to do today. It would be sad to see these advances thwarted before we have an opportunity to solidify them during the next few sessions." (Notice how the pastor anticipates the possibility of trouble. This is realistic and will keep them from thinking that their case is unusual or hopeless if trouble does arise.)

Howard: "Pastor, that's exactly what I'm afraid of. We may make a worse mess of things than ever before. I'm not sure we can hold our tongues for a week. I *expect* trouble."

Marcia: "I agree. You know we both have bad tempers; I'm sure we will raise all sorts of issues with one another. . . ."

P. "I don't expect the first week to be any picnic either; that's why I warned you to walk on eggs."

H. "If I know us, we'll be throwing them!"

P. "Tell me how you have handled problems in the past."

M. "Badly."

P. "But, *specifically,* what does that mean?" (Notice how the pastor will not settle for abstractions but insists on specific, concrete detail.)

H. "It means, pastor, that whenever a problem arises that we don't know how to solve, or that we disagree about how to solve, we get into a fight."

P. "What kind of fight—physical? Verbal?" (Notice, the pastor is still unwilling to settle for inexact data. Most counselors would let it go with the vague word "fight." He won't. The reason is that the two kinds of fights he distinguishes require different preventive measures. And if Howard were to respond "physical," he would continue to inquire about the kinds of physical abuses that have been experienced. It would be important to do so because if there was any physical danger to Marcia, he would want to guard against that.)

M. "Verbal."

H. "Yea, verbal. We've never slugged one another yet."

P. "How do you deal with these disagreements? Do you have any method at all? What I mean is, do you sit down and talk them out? Do you write out pros and cons? Do you go to the Bible for answers? . . . or what?" (Notice, once again he is probing for details that he doesn't have. The initial survey did not turn up adequate data to work with. He knows that assignments that he gives must deal with concrete facts, not abstractions. And, if there is a method already in use, or if the Bible is being used wrongly, he recognizes that he will have to deal with these abuses, or they themselves could occasion problems.)

H. "No, that's just the problem. There isn't any method in anything that we do. In fact, if we tried to decide on a method, we'd probably end up having a fight over that. We. . . ."

M. "Yes, all we do is get upset when we can't agree, and so we start yelling at each other, blaming one another for not agreeing, being the cause of the difficulty, and so on. We bring up nasty memories from the past and that is it. Howard's right; we don't have a method, but we need one. It was during one fight just like that, about discipline of the children, that Howard left. I don't want that to happen again."

H. "No, I don't either; but I'm afraid we won't be able to control ourselves if a problem does arise. Then where would we be?"

P. "Well, I guess you'd be in a mess, but that wouldn't be hopeless, of course. Next week, I want to begin to work with you on how to put into practice the biblical principles of communication and problem-solving, so that you *will* have a method. But you are telling me that you're afraid of the week between. Don't you think that you can, as I have said, walk on eggs for just one week in the meanwhile?" (Notice how the pastor gives realistic hope pointing to next week. He does not want them to get the mistaken notions that new patterns can be put on instantly or that everything can be explained at once, but he does look forward to new and better things.)

H. "I'm afraid to try."

M. "Me too. I can see eggs splattered all over us by the time the next session rolls around. What we need is a temporary method for dealing with problems that may arise *this* week."

P. "Mmmmmmm. Marcia, I think you've hit on it. Let's make an agreement right now about what to do about any unsolvable problems that do arise this week. I won't have time to instruct you thoroughly in the biblical principles and practices of communication and problem-solving today."

H. "Good."

P. "Howard, on the way home from here, buy a pad of paper. As soon as you get home, put it in the middle of the table along with a pen or pencil. Now, whenever a problem arises, and either one of you thinks you might be getting angry rather than solving it, you are to call a halt to any discussion that is going on and write out the problem on the pad. Then, bring the pad with you next week, and we'll discuss the problems on it under controlled circumstances and show you how God wants you to handle them as Christians. We'll use the pad as a casebook to which we can apply the principles I want to teach you. How does that strike you?''

M. ''I think that will help a lot. That way, we won't ignore the problem or hold it in or fight about it.''

H. ''Right.''

P. ''Well, for a *temporary* way to deal with most of your problems by helping you to 'pursue peace' instead of fighting, I think it will do very well.''

There you see how review of more general material led to a creative adaptation of the biblical command to ''pursue peace.'' The pastor's questioning and insistence on concrete detail rather than acceptance of mere generalization, led to a further discussion of how Marcia and Howard fight. Their P.D.I.[1] said merely, ''After a fight, Howard walked out on me.'' Up until then, the bulk of the counseling session had been devoted to bringing about forgiveness and reconciliation and an agreement to start living together again. That took more than a full hour. It would have been wrong for the counselor to get involved in anything deeper in this session. The two had come a long way already. There had been no time to delve into the statement on the P.D.I. in detail, or into a number of other things that the pastor had already listed on his agenda sheet.[2] So, in order to meet what he saw to be a genuine need, the pastor took time at the close of the session to suggest caution. (Insight into the possibility of their messing things up after the first session was again a matter of routine. It happens so often that competent counselors always warn against it and urge precaution.) Sometimes, as in this case, precautionary measures must be taken. In the dialog that you have read, you saw how the pastor discovered that warning alone would probably not be sufficient. But, in order to develop some temporary plan for handling problems, it was necessary for him to take enough time to discover some concrete facts out of which those creative preventive measures could be taken. He relied on *review* as the means for quickly leading him into the

1. See my book, *Update on Christian Counseling*, vol. I.
2. For details on note-taking, see the *Manual*, pp. 263ff.

areas that he must go, and it was successful. Under the pressure of necessity a creative suggestion, which could make all of the difference in the world to the couple in this case, was forthcoming. Of course, the pastor, like the reader of this page, now has this suggestion as a part of his counseling "past," which he can use "as is" or with adaptation to future cases. Creative adaptation of the general principles involved in the solution would yield countless variations. These variations would be needed when creatively adapting the solution to different situations.

For instance, if a wife always hits her husband in the face with an enumeration of the day's problems as he walks through the door, she might instead, out of consideration and love, write them down on a pad and place them beneath her husband's evening newspaper for him to read when he has had time to unwind after fighting the traffic on his way home from work. Instead of trying to remember all that happened (the reason she recited them all at once in the first place), she can now relax about that and focus on greeting him at the door with a cheery greeting and kiss. The common elements are the pad and the delayed action, together with the preservation of data and assurance that problems will be neither overlooked nor ignored. The unique elements are the application of this basic solution to quite a different situation—the location of the pad, its more permanent use, and the person writing. Placing the pad beneath the newspaper indicates an order of priority that the husband certainly will respect. Of course, the arrangement is best done by prior agreement in a counseling session if the husband is likely to respond negatively to use of the pad. Here, in counseling, its meaning, purpose, and use can be thoroughly explained and an agreement to use it can be reached. This will forestall any bad surprises. Moreover, when the husband gets the greeting and kiss, and then actually finds the pad beneath his newspaper, he knows what is going on and recognizes that his wife has been working on, and successfully dealing with, her problem. This concretely demonstrates love on her part and progress in handling the problem.

Reviewing can do many other things to help stimulate creativity. Not only does reviewing unearth new data, or give you a new slant on old data, but if, in reviewing, data are *restated in a new form*, especially when this new form involves the use of a figure of speech,[3] that form or language may itself trigger creativity. Figurative language and creativity are kissing cousins: when one thinks figuratively, he is already thinking creatively—particularly if he originates the figure, or even if he uses an old one (like "kissing cousins") consciously (that is, if he is aware of the meaning of the figure). Let's now look at another case that demonstrates something of this.

In this case, a counselor is wondering what is the best way to get Bill to curb his temper when, suddenly, he begins to think more literally about that figure of speech he has been using in his own mind. "Curb!" he exclaims. "That's it!" A curb is a raised area that runs along the side of the street to keep whatever belongs there (cars, water, etc.) in the street and off the sidewalk and people's lawns. A temper involves anger that is like a stream of water or cars, that needs side boundaries to channel it in the direction God wants it to take. "What we want, Bill, isn't a way to *block* your energy, but a way to direct it so that it heads in the right direction, toward proper, biblical goals. Even righteous anger, aroused for the right reasons, can be expressed sinfully when it has no curbs to keep it from driving all over others' lawns. Anger turns to temper when it bursts out of God's boundaries. We must curb that anger and channel it toward the constructive goal of problem-solving rather than tearing people apart, about which God speaks in Ephesians 4:29:

> Don't let a single rotten word come from your mouths, but rather, whatever is good for constructively meeting problems that arise, so that your words may help those who hear.

Let's see now what you can use as curbs. . . ." And off they go in search of some factors that will help Bill to channel his anger "constructively" to meet "problems that have arisen."

Saying the same thing in a new way can ring the bell.[4] You see this

---

3. Figurative language lends itself to creative thinking because it arouses pictures in the mind. Often, the creative implementation of a biblical precept results from the literalizing of figures of speech.

4. A figurative expression that itself could be literalized for a counseling situation in which every time someone does or says something that ought to be encouraged, a bell could literally be rung, or at least a word could be spoken that would approximate the same thing. Cf. the conference table, *Competent to Counsel*, pp. 231-36.

happening in the Scriptures themselves as the writers, by the expressions they use, often stimulate themselves to a more creative and fuller explanation of a point. That the Holy Spirit who superintended the writing of the Scriptures, so that they were produced without error, approved of the creative expression of thought in this way seems obvious. If you peruse the pages of an Epistle, you will be struck again and again by the process at work.

Let's take an example. In Ephesians 6:10, Paul uses the words "strong" and "strength" and speaks of God's "might." These words, in turn, suggest to him the idea of "armor" (v. 11), which itself leads him to creatively skewer together (a useful figure too) exhortations to faith, prayer, etc., under the extended figure of the full armor of God, as he begins to enumerate its pieces. Again, it was a figure of speech that made it possible to give the series of exhortations a form that was both coherent and memorable.

In the midst of a counseling session, especially when reviewing data, begin to listen for figures of speech that the counselee uses or that come to *your* mind. They are already creative in nature and, if explored (even picturesque words like this can become the source of creative thought: picture the explorer cutting the underbrush, etc.), frequently suggest creative adaptations of principles.

When perplexed or baffled, therefore, always review your data orally together with your counselees. The counselee himself may be the one to provide the creative clue as he says the same thing that he said before, but in a different way.

Let us say that you are sure that more must be done about structuring Barbara's daily life to keep her from brooding over the loss of her husband in self-pity. While reviewing her daily routine, you say, "Tell me once more what you do every day after you eat lunch. It seems, from the D.P.P. form[5] that it is usually in the afternoons that this problem crops up."

B.   "That's right, pastor. As I told you before, I seem to have the most difficulty during the time when I sit there opposite his chair. It's then that. . . ."

---

5. Discovering Problem Patterns form. For directions about its use, see the *Manual,* pp. 125, 192ff.

P.   "Wait a minute, Barbara; that's the first time I've heard you mention Matt's chair. Do you also sit in *'your* chair,' where the two of you used to sit and talk every afternoon before he died?"

B.   "Why, yes. . . ."

P.   "And then do you begin picturing[6] things the way they used to be?"

B.   "I guess so."

P.   "Have you rearranged any of the furniture in the house since your husband died three years ago?"

B.   "No."

P.   "*Everything* is the same?"

B.   "Yes."

P.   "Well, Barbara, you should begin to rearrange today. Things can never be the same again; God doesn't want them to be. You must arrange your house for the realities of the present, not for the memories of the past. Memories have their place, but we can't live in them. The failure to rearrange your house for the use of one person rather than two is unrealistic and perpetuates your problem because it tends to deny the facts. Now, first of all, you can have the boy next-door take Matt's chair to the attic. I think that it would be wise to leave it there for a while. And then. . . ."

Many other such ideas are suggested by the careful review of data. As you review, you will discover them. Creativity can be stimulated more easily, perhaps, by review than in any other way.[7]

Let us now turn to the second R.

Reverse It

If you ordinarily put it on the top, then try putting it on the bottom; if it heads west, then why not turn it toward the east? If something ordinarily is done on the inside, then do it on the outside. Whatever it is that you are working with, front/back, old/new, one side/other side, ask, "Will

---

6. He might have picked up on this figure, had he cared to, and talked about retouching the picture, painting a new one, etc.

7. But the counselor must expect to find creative solutions or he will not be on the lookout for them. Half the battle is won when you know how creativity can be stimulated and then expectantly watch for it.

reversing it help?'' Turn it on rather than turning it off, pull it rather than push it. Creativity is easily stimulated by reversals.

But, there is more to the reversal, in counseling, than in the stimulation of creativity. More often than not, in a world of sin, proper action calls for a complete reversal of whatever was wrong.

If Mark has been unsuccessful in convincing his wife that his repentance is genuine, then why not show her that it is not ingenuine? If Walt wants to find out what his gifts are, but seems confused by a mass of data, one place to begin is by eliminating those areas in which he obviously is not gifted. Something like this is suggested by Romans 12:3:

> Now, but the grace given to me, I tell every one of you: Don't think more highly of yourself than you ought to, but think soberly according to the measure of faith that God distributed to each of you.

If it is true that one cannot conquer fear directly, then why not overcome it indirectly by focusing on and cultivating the love that casts out fear? All of these approaches have one thing in common, no matter how they may otherwise differ: they use the principle of reversal in some way or another.

The biblical put off/put on dynamic (for a thorough explanation of which you should see appropriate places in the *Manual*) is built on the principle of reversal. And the overcoming of evil by doing good, rather than returning the same in kind (Rom. 14:12), is also a reversal pattern. Again, for details on the latter half of Romans 12, see my exposition and practical application of the passage in *How to Overcome Evil*.

Much in our sinful society, including many of the popular mores, customs, values, and ideals, require a complete reversal. God Himself put it this way:

> Let the wicked forsake his way and the unrighteous man his schemings; let him return to the Lord, and He will have mercy on him, to our God, for He will abundantly pardon. For My thoughts are not your thoughts, neither are My ways your ways, says the Lord (Isa. 55:7, 8, Berkeley).

The truth of these words can be seen through all of life. A depressed person, for instance, thinks that he cannot fulfill his responsibilities because he feels so depressed, when the truth of the matter is that h. feels bad *because* he has stopped assuming his God-given responsibilities. He has it backwards.

When we forsake our thoughts, they must be *replaced* by God's thoughts; we must learn to think God's thoughts after Him; and then we must learn to walk in the ways that He walked in Jesus Christ. We must make His thoughts and ways ours. When we do, more often than many would suppose, we shall see that a complete reversal of thought and of action is what is necessary. For that reason, one of the first creative thoughts that a counselor might think is, "What action, thought, or pattern is the opposite or the reversal of this counselee's sinful one?" Consider these: lying/truth telling, stealing/hard work and giving (Eph. 4:25, 28).

Many more examples might be cited to illustrate various aspects of the point, but as one carefully examines the antithetical nature of John's writings (belief/unbelief, light/darkness, truth/lying, life/death, love/ hate), he can understand why reversal is so important a consideration in counseling.

Now, let's take a case. Phil has been acting strangely lately, in ways that he had never been before. First, he became extremely irritable, then suspicious of his family and friends, and finally, he went berserk. Responses from those around him made it clear that he had hardly slept at all for the better part of a week. Now that he has caught up on his sleep loss, under his counselor's advice, he has been acting normally again. The counselor explains to him that sleep loss in some persons can lead to every effect of LSD. The bizarre behavior resulting from sleep loss was but a complicating problem. Then, after dealing with the problems that led to the sleep loss, the counselor isolated all of the patterns they could discover in Phil's life that might lead to sleep loss. Next he helped Phil draw up an entirely new daily schedule, one that reversed the old patterns leading to sleep loss and its debilitating effects. He reversed his rising time from a late to an early one, as well as his study from late night to early morning and afternoon; and his night owl friendships were replaced by new friendships with early birds.

Because this reversal dynamic is so obvious once one becomes aware of it, I shall not belabor the point. But do not neglect it because it seems so simple. Because of sin, often the most creative thing to do is simply to shift into reverse and back out of the problem.

Revise It

Of course, everything I have suggested thus far entails revision. But what I refer to here is modification, substitution, adaptation, and alteration in some way other than by complete reversal. Not all patterns need to be or can be reversed.

When the rich young ruler came to Jesus, our Lord corrected him. He told him, "There is no one who is good but God." His words and his thinking were challenged in a way that was designed to alter both. When a Christian counselee says, "It's hopeless," his counselor should answer, "What God says is that it is *difficult;* but it is not hopeless." He may need to explain I Corinthians 10:13 to him at that point. He alters his perspective by correcting his language and the thinking that it generates. When a counselee, echoing the world, says, "Well, I guess honesty is the best policy," a counselor will reply, "God says honesty is the *only* policy." That is an important revision. Perhaps as we take a look at a case or two we shall see creative adaptation at work more clearly.

One of the most frequent errors that counselees make is in attempting to judge motives. Nearly always their judgment is wrong, and this very judgment becomes the occasion for suspicion, division, and anger. The Bible explicitly teaches that "man looks on the outward appearance" and that God alone can look on the "heart." (In the Bible, the word "heart" does not mean feelings, but it means *inner life*—the life one lives before God and himself alone.) We may not judge hearts. It is very important, then, to get counselees to stop judging the motives of others' hearts and to start judging their words and actions instead. That modification of thought and action can be revolutionary in its effects. Consider a very simple case:

Beverly's mother was having a hard time with this. Beverly, a 14-year-old, was beginning to grow up. Actually, she was not involved in drugs, illicit sex, or any other sinful pursuits, but she had begun to use the language of her peers. For some reason, her mother focused on her use of "yeah" rather than "yes." Mother was distressed by this change in her daughter's vocabulary. She seemed to think of it as a symbol of other things far worse, and began to make judgments about Beverly that were totally unwarranted. She began to attribute all sorts of inner motives to her that were simply bad judgments, based on guesswork rather than on facts. The counselor pointed out the error of her ways and was able to help her to modify her approach. However, he did not say "stop making judgments," as some do; this was not a matter of reversal. Instead, he commended her for her concern for her daughter and her willingness to make judgments, but he insisted that she "judge a righteous judgment." He said, "You have every right to make judgments. Indeed, you *must* do so. And it is right to judge Beverly's language and her actions. But you may not judge her *heart*. Only God has the right to do that, and only He *can* do that. Focus on those two outer things, instead of motives and thoughts, and you will begin to get somewhere."

That change of direction and of attention, seemingly small, but large in its effects, made a world of difference in the relationship between mother and daughter. Mom stopped trying to second-guess what was going on in Beverly's mind and worked on objectionable language and behavior alone. When she wanted to know what Beverly was thinking, she *asked* her. As a result, she stopped letting her imagination run wild. Beverly, on the other hand, was so happy not to be accused of thinking and doing things that were not true that she was glad to work on her speech habits.

Take another entirely different situation. Jan and Jimmy had been having bad sexual relations and this had been a point of contention that threatened their marriage. "It seems as if we have no feelings for each other any more," they say. "The more we work on the problem, the less successful we are. There isn't much in it for either of us these days." After extensive data gathering, and discussion of the *whole* of their marriage relationship, the counselor said,

> I think you have looked at sexual relations as something apart from the rest of your lives. Good sexual relations begin when you crawl out of the covers in the morning, not when you slip between the sheets at night. If you have bad interpersonal relations all day long and don't resolve those problems before you get into bed at night, you carry all of that baggage to bed with you. The Bible teaches in Ephesians 4 that you must not let the sun go down on your anger. Deal with these other problems and I think your sexual problems will

also begin to clear up. After all, can you have good sexual relations in a bed piled high with suitcases? Get rid of the baggage that you put there all day long before you crawl into bed, and you will have plenty of room for sexual activity.

This change in focus, pictured vividly so that they would remember it, helped Jan and Jimmy to solve their problem. Modification and substitution, i.e., a shift in emphasis from the mechanics of sexual relations to the dynamics of interpersonal relations, brought about the change.

One more example must be enough for this chapter, which has already grown too long. Herb asks, "Pastor, how can I find marriage fulfilling?" He then goes on to detail facts concerning a marriage in which his complaint is that Jane has "failed to meet his needs for companionship." Jane, in response says, "From my side of the relationship, I could make the very same complaint." In providing help, the pastor turns the spotlight on the real problem. He begins by pointing out the basic flaw in their thinking: "You are both thinking only of what you can *get* out of marriage; that is the wrong approach. Love is concerned about giving, not about getting. It gives with no thought of what will be returned. It asks, 'How can I fulfill my partner? How can I provide companionship for him/her?' not 'What can he/she do for me?' "

So far, the pastor has been using reversal. But, he continues, "You must have a biblical priority on your agenda. From what you have said, you will have to make some changes by replacing thoughts of getting with thoughts of giving. Now, it isn't wrong for either of you to want to help the other to assume his or her responsibilities, even when they are responsibilities that he/she exercises on your behalf. Yet, it would be wrong to put that at the top of your priority list. Instead, let's see what a *revised* list of priorities for marriage might look like.

"First, as top priority, should be the goal of pleasing God by being the companion that He wants you to be, whether you find that your partner expresses appreciation for your efforts or not, and whether or not he/she does the same. Second on the list would be providing help for the partner to assume his/her responsibilities. Your concern here should be to help him/her to honor God by becoming what he/she should be in the marriage. When you have these things straight and are honestly willing to do all you can from that commitment, you will find that *as a byproduct* (but you can't do it as a gimmick for this reason) you will also begin to enjoy marriage more. In this, as in every other application of that important principle, you will discover that 'it is more blessed to give than to receive.' "

After reversal, there was still the necessity to *revise* by rearranging the priorities by which they were operating. They needed a revised agenda that fitted their new biblical understanding of marriage, which is a covenant of companionship (for more on that point, see the first section of my book, *Marriage, Divorce and Remarriage in the Bible*).

So, be a revisionist! Look at the facts again, and again, and perfect the plan. A good writer writes and rewrites until he gets it right. So too, creativity is often just a matter of plain, hard work, going over and over something until you see exactly what must be done and how. In revision, one sees the old way from a different perspective, in a new light, or from a different vantage point. He views what has been done from his stance on the Bible and looks toward what God wants done instead.

Revision means working to rearrange, reorient, rework, or refine[8] something until it fits the biblical requirement snugly. It will often take not only rough work, but fine polishing as well to make it fit rightly. So understood, revision usually falls at the end of the three-step process for stimulating creative responses to counselee problems. Sticking close to these three Rs—reviewing, reversing, and revising—you will go a long way toward providing a simple but profound working method by which to become creative and by which to continue to develop your abilities until you become expert at it.

---

8. Note that all of these words begin with the prefix *re*, which means "again."

12

REVIEW IT

Let's do a little reviewing ourselves. In other words, we'll go back over the territory and try to come at the question of creativity another way. I shall ask again, "How does one develop creativity?" and see what sort of answer we can come up with this time. One way to reply is to say, "Creativity is developed by those who become convinced that there is a possibility for them to develop creativity." They, and they alone, are the ones who do. Another response may be, "Creativity is developed by those who conscientiously pursue creativity." Obviously, the how-to in the previous chapters will be of little value unless the counselor (1) is convinced that there is a possibility for him to become a creative person and then (2) makes every genuine effort to do those things that are necessary to cultivate creativity. Good intentions and right theoretical positions alone will not get the job done. Now, taking this view of the matter opens several further considerations.

Until a counselor sees the pertinence of creativity to counseling, along with its importance and necessity, he will not be highly motivated to expend the necessary time and effort to pursue it. The development of skills is costly. Skills can never be had free. They can be acquired only by conscious, disciplined, persistent, prayerful effort. No counselor is going to devote time out of an already crowded schedule to the pursuit of creativity unless he earnestly believes that good counseling is dependent upon it. It is my opinion that in such matters motivation is directly proportional to the *amount of use* that the counselor thinks he will make of creativity. After all, we have no direct biblical command, "Thou shalt become creative" (although Heb. 10:24 comes very close to it). Therefore, a Christian must become convinced that developing creativity is one of the ways of enabling him to "stimulate others to love and fine deeds."

Nor is he likely to dedicate himself to the acquisition of creative skills when he doesn't believe it is possible for *him* to acquire them. No matter how valuable he may think that they would be, and no matter how much he may want them, he will expend absolutely no effort if he believes that effort would be fruitless. Any such pursuit would amount to an exercise in futility. If, therefore, he holds the erroneous view that creativity is the prerogative of a privileged few, in whom the capacity for creativity is inborn, again there will be little incentive unless he thinks he is among that privileged cast.

And, so long as a counselor is unwilling to make the conscientious efforts that are necessary to acquire creative skills, because of ignorance, laziness, lack of concern (love), fear, or whatever, he will fail to become very creative. This is true because, as Hebrews 10:24 makes very clear, the pursuit of proper ways and means for "stimulating others to love and fine deeds" is something that requires the strenuous effort of "putting one's mind down to it" (*katanoeo*). (The word for stimulating others also is a strong term that in some contexts ought to be translated "provoke, irritate, or goad. Such stimulation itself, therefore, can be difficult and taxing.) To "put one's mind down to" consideration of ways of helping others means to give careful contemplation, research, and study of ways and means. Involved in that, necessarily, is study of creativity itself.

Furthermore, even if one puts all sorts of time, thought, and effort into the pursuit of creativity, his best intentions will fail if they are misdirected. It is the pursuit of *correct* practices, directed by biblical principles, alone that succeeds.

So then, in summary, we may say that the acquisition of counseling creativity depends on four factors:

1. Recognition of the importance of creativity to counseling
2. Belief in the possibility of acquiring creative skills
3. Conscientious effort and prayer in pursuing creativity
4. Pursuit of correct practices

I have dealt with the first two factors already. The third, in the final analysis, is a matter of one's own personal relationship to God. Overcoming laziness, lack of love, etc., is not a matter of acquiring skills; it is a matter of repentance. There must be a willingness to recognize sin for what it is and a desire to live differently in the future. It is not the design of this book to deal with that problem, though I do not mean in omitting it to imply that it is a problem that is either unimportant or always easy to handle. Quite to the contrary; it is so vital and would therefore require so much time and space that I could not be expected to handle it here because it would take us too far afield. I shall assume that for the reader it is not a problem. So, that leaves us with the fourth factor to consider further: What are the correct practices that, if faithfully pursued, inevitably will lead to skill in creative thought and action?

Obviously, what we have been doing already is considering this matter. But, from a different perspective, I want to reconsider the question. So far, we have discussed analysis and synthesis and the three Rs. In this chapter, I want to take a closer look at the concept of *newness*, which is at the heart of the creative process, to see what part it plays in the development of creative skills.

We have seen that newness is an integral part of creativity. But let us ask, what is newness? In the Greek New Testament there are two terms for newness: *kainos* and *neos* (etymologically, our English word *new* is related to *neos*).

The first word, *kainos*, has to do with newness in respect to form or quality. It means "fresh," "unused," or "novel" (*brand* new). The other word, *neos*, has to do with time and means "young" or "recent." In English, because we do not have two words for these varied concepts, we must substitute or add words to indicate such things. We must say "fresh" or "young" or say "brand-new" or "new to me." To say, "I have a new car" in English, for instance, is indefinite. In order to be sure of your meaning, someone may ask, "Is the car brand-new or only new to you?" So, when we speak of newness as integral to creativity, which do we mean? Without further definition the statement is ambiguous and could be taken either way by different persons.

The basic concern in creativity is not with newness in the sense of recency or youth. But very much to the point is newness as *freshness*. Fresh ideas and practices that also are new to either the counselee or the counselor, or both, are precisely what is needed.

Consider the Greek words *e kine diatheke*, which means, "The New Testament." The point is not merely that the New Testament or Covenant is the latest in time or most recent (*neos*). That is beside the point, even though many people, perhaps most, think wrongly that this is the import of the word *new*. That wrong idea is the result of this confusion in English that flows from the fact that we have only one English word for newness to do the service of two that appear in the Greek New Testament.

Rather, what those words indicate is that there is a *brand-new* (fresh) covenant. The covenant that Jeremiah predicted, and about which the entire set of books called the New Covenant speaks, is a fresh one—different in nature. That is, of course, the very point that was emphasized by Jeremiah when predicting the coming of the new covenant: "I will make a new covenant . . . *not like the covenant* that I made with their fathers" (Jer. 31:31, 32). Then, in the verses that follow, Jeremiah contrasts the ways in which the two covenants differ. The Book of Hebrews might well serve as a commentary on those differences.

Of course, the differences do not imply that there is nothing but disjunction between the two covenants; there is also continuity. In fact, the new is the fulfillment of the old. The new is the reality of which the old spoke in types and symbols and shadows. As a matter of fact, it is a new (fresh or different) administration of the one overarching covenant of grace. By that covenant, God saves all those who come to Him in repentance for sin and with faith in His Son, the Lord Jesus Christ our Savior. He, as the perfect, once-for-all, vicarious, substitutionary sacrifice for sins, was the reality that all of the old covenant sacrifices pictured and to which they pointed. So, it is a newness like the kind of newness that we have already been confronting in this book, where old things take on new meanings, where the brand-new is, nevertheless, a brand-newness that comes from new constructions of the old. The newness of which the Bible speaks grows out of and is built on the old.

In Revelation 21 we read of a *kainos* heavens and a *kainos* earth to which a *kainos* Jerusalem comes down. All of these are new, again, in that same sense. They are new, in that there has never been anything exactly like them before, but they still may be called a *heavens* and an *earth* and a *city* of *Jerusalem*. Those four words, once more, demonstrate the continuity in diversity that we are encountering. The difference is so great that they can be called fresh, brand-new; but not *so* great that they are something entirely other.

In all creativity in counseling, likewise we must use old concepts, plans, etc., in new ways. We are not calling for something so diverse that it comes out of the sky; what we want is fresh approaches. Unlike God, human beings cannot create *de novo* (out of nothing). We must work from old concepts to fresh ones. But, since the original *de novo* creation, God Himself has worked in the same way, molding the new out of the old, and will continue to do so in the future (only, of course, so much more powerfully than we can). That means that we can learn something about creativity from His re-forming and redoing activities as well.

When the new heavens and earth are formed, Peter tells us, the old will be melted down and purified, and a *kainos* heavens and earth will be brought into existence out of what emerges from the conflagration. Old materials will be reformed and remolded into fresh ones bearing no traces of sin or its effects, but yet, being identifiable as *heavens* and *earth,* thus having continuity with the old. The new will be a remade, reworked, perfect version of the old. Similarly, the new, resurrected body will be a fresh, perfect version of the former one; but it too will have continuity with the old in likeness and in some way in substance. And, when the regenerated believer in this life is called a " new *(kainos)* creation" (II Cor. 5:17), it is a creation that is like the creation of the new heavens and earth (cf. Gal. 6:15, where *kainos* also is used).[1] The "new man" that one becomes in Christ is a remaking of the old sinful human who is regenerated. And, finally, in New Testament times, the church is composed of both Jews and Gentiles, making this combined body "one *kainos* person" (Eph. 2:15). Clearly old elements are combined in *new ways.*

The whole New Testament period, as well as the age to come, may be said to be *kainos.* It is fresh, brand-new, when compared with the old era and the sinful world with which it contrasts. For something to be *kainos,* then, means that it is new in a positive sense. It is qualitatively different in a good sense. This newness is superior, better (see the Book of Hebrews on this), or more valuable. That, too, is the idea in newness in creative counseling: A better way to deal with the problem must be

---

1. Isaiah speaks of this "creation" of a new heavens and earth *and* Jerusalem in 65:17, 18, using *bara* in the lesser sense of the term (not as creation out of nothing). The sense in which *bara* is used is made clear in Isa. 66:22, where the new heavens and earth are said to be *made (asah)*; this Hebrew term is used for construction, building, where material is in view.

found. Kittel says, "In the NT *kainos* means not yet used . . . and unusual." To be creative, then, is to find or to produce unusual ways of applying and implementing biblical solutions to problems; ways that have not yet been tried (at least) by the counselor or the counselee in question.

Indeed, as I think that you have begun to see, the concept of *kainos* newness runs throughout the New Testament Scriptures, indicating that this is a *kainos* era in which for Christians all things, including counseling, are to be characterized by their *kainos* quality. Living the *kainos* life, therefore, is living a different—creatively different—sort of existence from the sort of life unregenerate persons experience. Unregenerate persons have no contact with the *kainos* Man, Jesus Christ, and do not have His *kainos* life within them. They know little or nothing of the power of the *kainos* age to come. One of the great tragedies in the unregenerate person's life is that for him there truly is nothing new under the sun. Life soon grows old, stale; he knows nothing of that freshness of God's mercies which are new every morning. Because he has never undergone the transforming power of Christ, he does not know what true freshness of life is all about. Even his best creative efforts (and, of course, he too is able to exercise this creative capacity that God built into human life) fall short. They are always ruined, destroyed, twisted and warped by sin (Prov. 14:13). In the long run, they prove meaningless to him, and the very uses to which he puts them are meaningless, warped, or even harmful. What must the creative minds that discovered nuclear power think about their discovery when, in their better moments, they recognize the potential for world destruction they have placed in the hands of so many men who have proven to be anything but responsible persons.

On the contrary, because he has a *kainos* life, is in touch with *kainos* power, and is in possession of a *kainos* revelation, the Christian is capable of truly fresh thought and action.

Yet, in spite of this fact, it is Christians who are often so much less creative than some of their unregenerate counterparts (who at least see the need for creativity and work hard at it, with, of course, the tragic and dissatisfying outcomes I have already described). Christians ought to be known for their satisfying, joyous, creative outlook on life; they should be known for their positive innovations and for their contributions to the thought and life of society. In counseling, they should not *follow* the secular pack, mimicking them; rather they should be seen as innovative and trend-setting. That they have not been accounts for much of the dull, lackluster and tiresome sameness that plagues the church, and for the existence in society at large of such confusion in the counseling field that it may hardly be called anything short of chaos. It is time for the church to awaken to the untapped *kainos* potential that she has and to become truly *kainos* in all of her activities.

This creative activity, full of vivacity, freedom, and buoyancy,[2] is, however, not a lawless thing. The principles and practices of *kainos* living are found in the Bible. Therefore, counselors must learn how to be creative *within* the biblical framework, according to biblical commands and patterns.

But doesn't this bind? Doesn't this put a damper on creativity? Won't freedom of thought and activity be hampered by such confining strictures?

No, exactly not so. It is these principles and practices that, because of their *kainos* nature and orientation, become the impetus for and give the direction to creativity that is truly *kainos*. They put meaning into creativity; they provide the materials of thought that can be creatively adapted and implemented in counseling. That which is truly fresh, unique, and satisfying can be only the fruit of *kainos* activity. Because the Christian counselor possesses the *kainos* Scriptures and is activated in living the *kainos* life by the Spirit of holiness, it is not only possible for him to become creative in every good sense of the word, it is *mandatory*.

The biblical principles according to which he counsels are of two sorts. First, there are direct commands and examples: "The thief must stop stealing . . ." (Eph. 4:28); "Be imitators of me as I am of Christ" (I Cor. 11:1). Secondly, there are more general injunctions and indications: "give thought to ways of stimulating one another to love and to fine deeds" (Heb. 10:24). I keep returning to this verse because I think it

2. The *kainos* man is also to have a *neos* (youthful) attitude that corresponds to this. In Eph. 4:23, the spirit (or attitude of mind) that leads to *kainos* life (the life of the *new* man who replaces the old) is one that is being made "youthful" (*ananoeo*). This youthful spirit should characterize the Christian's thinking. The word "created" in v. 23 must refer, as we have seen in previous contexts, to creation out of existing things rather than to creation *de novo*. It is the fresh righteousness and holiness of the *kainos* life that is in view.

is very important for counselors. It refers, of course, to all Christians, not only to those who do counseling as a part of their life calling. All the more reason, then, that those who are counselors in the more formal sense of the word should take heed to it.

The first two verses are more specific than the third. They give concrete directions (the first even more than the second), not only in the particular action to take but also by specifying something about how to do it. The third, in contrast, turns the reader loose to come up with ways and means that he has creatively developed for himself. The second verse, concerning imitation, sends the reader back to the biblical record of the life of Paul to investigate the ways he imitated his Lord. The third verse requires the reader to think up ways and means. They will not be provided for him in the Bible even as the second group of materials is. These ways and means, naturally, must be in accordance with biblical principles, must grow out of them, and at every point will be informed by them so that they will always be in complete harmony with them. Nevertheless, they will come about only by a youthful (*neos*) spirit, full of divinely given and sustained *kainos* vitality, brought to bear on the problems at hand. Even in implementing and applying the first two verses creativity will often be necessary. And, at that point the third verse also may come into play. For instance, *how* may a former thief best use his hands to earn money that he must give to those in need? At times, ways of creative thought about stimulating him to do so may also be necessary. But in any case, he must ask, "To which persons in need should I give the money I have earned with my own hands?" Then, he may ask, "How will I give? Anonymously? Can that be done 'in Christ's Name'?" And so on, and on, the questions may be asked; but all of them get into areas about which only more general principles are given. That means that the counselor will find it necessary to be creative even in such instances. The fact of particularity, of individuality, that is so much a part of counseling, screams out for creative adaptation.

We have seen, then, that there is a creative necessity for which God has prepared His people by giving them *kainos* life and power that, exercised within the framework of *kainos* principles and practices, enables them to be truly creative. There can be no excuse, therefore, either for the counselor or for the counselee to say "I cannot do it."

13

THE OLD AND THE NEW

In the previous chapter we saw that *kainos* thought and activity is in continuity with and grows out of the old. That means that the new is not a rejection of the old but a fulfilment and a further advance on it or an adaptation of it that is made in order to meet new circumstances. The new, in such cases, calls forth the new. Creativity is a response to new circumstances. As *kainos* activity remolds, remakes, and renews what was corrupted by sin, so in counseling, biblical solutions to problems used in promoting *kainos* living must correspondingly do the same. And the renewal, as I suggested in my book, *More than Redemption,* is more than a renewal of what formerly existed, even at its best in Eden. It is an advance upon it. Often, new circumstances stretch counselors and counselees, and promote growth, so that there is genuine advance in counseling practice as well as in the life of the counselee as the result of calling forth creative activity. Indeed, it is possible to say that *every* truly creative solution marks an advance for the counselor himself. That, then, is the way to think about creativity in counseling.

But, in making these remarks, I have used two biblical terms that might be considered more fully with profit. They are *renewal* and *fulfil.*

In speaking of the Old Testament books, with their teaching and practices, Jesus gave us this important warning:

> Don't think that I came to abolish the law or the prophets; I didn't come to abolish but to fulfil (Matt. 5:17).

What did He mean? The word for fulfil is *pleroo,* which also means "to fill, complete, accomplish, and to give something its true meaning" (Arndt and Gingrich). Christ fulfilled the law and the prophets by teaching and demonstrating their true meaning. He fulfilled them as the reality fulfils the type. He fulfilled them by accomplishing in His person all that they left undone, which pointed to His coming. In all of this we see continuity, not discontinuity, between the old and the new. Christ does not *abolish* but *fulfils.* The creative, *kainos* counselor does the same. He clears up misunderstandings, demonstrates true meanings, and leads counselees into successful accomplishments by creative explanations, applications, and implementations of biblical truth. That is what Christ did in the so-called Sermon on the Mount. I have written on this in my book, *Update on Christian Counseling,* vol. I:

The Practicality of the Sermon on the Mount

One fact that I have insisted on over the years (and have worked hard to rectify) is that conservative churches have been strong on the *what-to* (in both preaching and counseling—i.e., where they have done biblical counseling at all), but weak on the *how-to.*

I

In counseling I have discovered that many counselees are in serious trouble because, while they know *what* the Lord requires of them, they do not know *how* to go about meeting these requirements—no one ever told them. Indeed, many don't even know where to begin. Again and again in counseling sessions the breakthrough comes when I begin to apply known scriptural truths practically (concretely directing the counselee in the ways and means of kneading biblical principles into the dough of his life). That's when he comes alive and things begin to happen. Before, he knew what to do (at least generally, though sometimes this needs sharpening too); this he had been taught again and again (in Sunday School, from the pulpit, in Christian books). And usually I find that he has tried, only to fail again and again. Soon (characteristically) he gives up, saying, "Well, maybe Paul can do it, but I'm not Paul." This failure syndrome is widespread in the church.

The answer to the problem—as I have taught in all my books—is to begin to include the *how-to* in all counseling. When I caught on to this and began to focus on this in my counseling practice, I also began to see a tremendous difference in counseling results. If my past 14 years of counseling experience has demonstrated anything, it has pointed up the utter need for creative practicality in the *use* of the Scriptures.

Now, as I said, I have hammered away at this point, given many examples of what I mean and have taught others also how to use the

Scriptures practically (that doesn't exclude exegesis and theology, but rather seeks to achieve individual applications of both). But, as I scan my books, I notice that I have largely *assumed* that this was a biblical emphasis; I have not adequately supported that assumption from the Scriptures themselves. And, in question-and-answer periods this has been pointed out by various questions from time to time. So here I shall make one initial thrust that—in and of itself (I believe)—should establish this practice as biblical.

If, over the years, any unit of biblical material has been thought of as ''idealistic'' or ''impractical'' by those who do not believe or do not understand (or are unsympathetic with) its teachings, it has been the Sermon on the Mount. I propose, therefore, to examine this sermon (as it appears in the Gospel according to Matthew) to show (1) that the charge of impractical idealism cannot be sustained and (2) that the Scriptures clearly demonstrate that (in His preaching) Jesus was concerned equally with the *what-to* and the *how-to*. The Sermon on the Mount, I think you will agree (when I am through), is eminently practical. Moreover, along the way, I hope to discover some of the how-to for the development and use of how-to. So let us begin.

II

The first section of the Sermon on the Mount (Matt. 5:1-20) is introductory; it sets the stage for what follows. One would not expect much application in the introduction to a sermon. The beatitudes (which have very practical implications for life—someone has quipped, ''The beatitudes are the attitudes we ought to be at''—but these are not spelled out practically) give an exciting profile of what God's people may (indeed *must*) become. Here, in this list, are both their ideals and their hope. Then, in summarizing the influence that Christians like this may bear, Jesus says they must be salt (a preserving influence) and light (an illuminating, guiding influence). All these ideals are possible and may be realized, not by overthrowing the O.T. principles of living (vv. 17-19) but (unlike the scribes and Pharisees) by properly interpreting, applying and living according to those commandments in all their fulness (v. 20). This fulness would be described by Jesus in the sermon that follows and demonstrated by Him in the life He would live and the death He would die.

The phrase, "You have heard . . . but I say," refers not to the O.T. Scriptures—as though Jesus were abrogating God's principles of living taught there—but to the false scribal interpretations *and applications* (He takes up *both*[1] and, therefore, counters *both* with correct alternatives.) In the sections that follow, Jesus shows how to *interpret* and to *apply* the Scriptures properly. Naturally, he makes concrete, practical, *how-to* type applications in doing so. Even the conclusion to the sermon fits this analysis; it too is practical in emphasis: The Christian's righteousness will exceed the righteousness of the scribes and Pharisees when he learns *both* to *hear* and to *do* all Jesus commands.

N.B., Jesus lays emphasis upon *both* hearing and doing; He sees no place for truth unapplied and unappropriated. The what-to is not enough (in some ways, that was the Pharisee's problem: he knew the what-to, but he either failed to work it out in daily living, or did so in a perverted way); it must issue in practical Christian living.

Following the introduction, Jesus becomes practical and specific. First He takes up the sixth commandment, the one that prohibits murder (v. 21). The scribes had restricted its application to the limited circumstance of actual homicide. But Jesus makes it clear that the commandment is broad; He shows too that it has an inner application as well. Therefore, it includes unrighteous anger, and the expression of such anger in words. For instance, two Christians must never allow any matter to separate them because of anger. Bitterness and resentment may not come between them; they must be reconciled.

"But what happens when, in this world of sin, they do allow such things to come between them?" someone might ask. Jesus anticipates the situation, and (in very practical *how-to*—here even step-by-step— terms) He tells us *how to* handle the situation (vv. 23, 24). The practical how-to comes in the form of a procedure growing out of the priority of reconciliation. Clearly verses 23 and 24 are how-to verses.[2]

---

1. Most commentators have stressed the interpretations alone. The two can be distinguished but, of course, cannot be separated; the one supported the other.

2. Cf. Matt. 18:15ff.; Luke 17:3ff. for other step-by-step how-to directions about the same matter.

Next, Jesus makes a second application of the sixth commandment. Once again He shows exactly how it may be applied, this time, when dealing with an unbeliever. In a pending court trial, it is better not to let your anger keep you from doing the sensible thing—settling out of court, as quickly as possible. Otherwise, you may be sorry.

So, as Jesus discusses the sixth commandment, we note that He offers two case studies and recommends specific, concrete action, often in the form of steps (''First . . . then''). These are important principles for counselors to understand and follow.

But that is just the beginning. Next, He turns to the seventh commandment (vv. 27-30). Again, after broadening the commandment beyond the mere outward act to include the heart, He turns to how-to (vv. 29, 30). If one must not look on a woman lustfully, then (the question arises) *how* can he avoid doing so? He gives a concrete answer: by putting impediments in his way. Whatever member of the body has been offending (even a *right* eye, *right* hand, *right* foot—*right,* indicating the most important), it must be removed. Jesus never intended this to be understood literally. His point was, as mutilation would make it difficult to perform an act again, so whatever led to adultery (or any other sin) of the heart similarly must be removed. The truly repentant believer does not want to offend again, so (and this is the *how-to*) he will do all he can to make it difficult to fall into the same sin again.[3]

In verses 31 and 32, Jesus takes up another false interpretation that (again) leads to sinful action. Deuteronomy 24 was not intended to allow or institute divorce, but only to regulate it. In this case, the Pharisees had broadened a narrow O.T. passage to make it teach things that it was not designed to say. So, Jesus narrowed it once again to the correct interpretation (I cannot treat the many ramifications of the divorce/remarriage question here. I have tapes[4] available on the question and am writing a book on the subject). In the process, Christ clarifies the biblical position on divorce, the exception to it (among believers) and the results of violating the biblical position by misusing the Scriptures for one's own purposes. There is no *how-to* here, because the discussion is (essentially) negative;

---

3. For more on this, in detail, see my *Christian Counselor's Manual,* ch. 19.

4. Available from Christian Study Services, 1790 E. Willow Grove Ave., Laverock, Pa. 19118.

but there is plenty of how *not* to!

Turning to the next passage (vv. 33-37), Jesus tightens up another commandment that was being misused by the Jews. Their preoccupation was with the exact formula of oath-taking. By cleverly worded vows and oaths they could seem to swear when they didn't do so at all—or at least that's what *they* thought! Christ was concerned about honesty—being a man of one's word. One's reputation for honesty should be so stainless that his word alone is sufficient (he need not swear).[5] But the important fact, for our purposes, is the clear-cut how-to that Jesus gives. He teaches explicitly that one must solve the question of oaths *beforehand*, not afterward (v. 37—He must always mean yes when he says "yes" and no when he says "no"). Christians must stop playing word games altogether (vv. 34ff.). Simply, clearly, say yes or no and mean it. That is long-term, sweeping, but explicit how-to. It sliced through all the confusion, arguments, and sophistry. No casuistry was needed.

In verse 38, another issue is raised. The Christian's personal ethic must be distinguished from civil punishment (Paul picks up on this in Romans 12 and 13). As individuals, we must learn to respond with love, overcoming evil with good (for a full discussion of this see my *How to Overcome Evil*). Verses 39-42 are *how-to* verses—each explains *how* God wants Christians to handle pressure and persecution rather than retaliate. To help, again Jesus illustrates the how-to principles by cases that clearly might apply to actual situations that any one of them might face.

In verses 43-48, Jesus continues this basic theme: a Christian must *love* his enemies. But, unlike many modern preachers, Christ didn't leave the concept of love hanging in thin air—undefined and amorphous. Rather, He was quite specific: love focuses on the other person; not on one's self. Therefore (note the specific how-to) a Christian must pray for his enemies. That concrete proposal Paul developed (as we must develop all such suggestions) in Romans 12:14ff.

And so the sermon continues. There is no let-up on the practicality of the material confronted in chapter 6. Here, the general principle is set forth: Don't do righteousness for the approval of others, or that is *all* you

5. On this passage (and the entire sermon) see John R. Stott's excellent book, *The Christian Counter Culture* (Downer's Grove, Ill.: InterVarsity Press, 1978).

will get for your efforts. Jesus cites four areas of abuse (note how He works a principle into a number of practical situations):

1. Giving charity for personal acclaim (vv. 2-4);
2. Praying like the hypocrites (vv. 5, 6);
3. Praying like the pagans (vv. 7-15);
4. Fasting to exhibit humility to others (vv. 16-18).

To each of these four areas, Jesus appends some how-to advice that (if followed) will keep the Christian from falling into the traps just mentioned. Here it is:

Verse 3—Do your giving anonymously.

Verse 6—Pray regularly in a private place.

Verses 9-13—Pray briefly and to the point, listing distinct items in sequence, ridding prayer of all unnecessary repetition.

Verses 17, 18—Fasting before God alone.

Indeed, as you can see, even the so-called Lord's prayer was given (at this place) in order to show *how* to pray (cf. v. 9a). It is a how-to model.

The next section of the sermon (vv. 22-34) covers the interrelated sins of avarice and anxiety.The answer to avoiding these Siamese twins is stated in very practical terms (vv. 33, 34):

1. Set your priorities properly (v. 33);
2. Set you efforts and concern on solving today's (not tomorrow's) problems (v. 34).[6]

Chapter 7 continues along the same lines. What to do about judging is the theme of the first five verses in this chapter. Jesus not only sounds a warning against sinful forms of judging, but He lays out a concrete how-to procedure that (1) will prevent one from sinful judging and (2) will help him to judge righteously (v. 5). In modern terms, the how-to principle may be stated this way: Put the lid on your own garbage can before complaining about the odor from someone else's.

Though this discussion has been brief and summary, I think it is perfectly clear by this point that Christ was concerned about how-to as well at what-to. Without detailing the rest, notice how-to instructions (continuing throughout chapter 7) in verse 7 (ask if you want something), verse 12 (treat others as you'd want them to treat you), and verse 16 (you

6. Verse 34 has been unpacked in a pamphlet, *What to Do About Worry;* verse 33 could (likewise) be treated much more fully.

can discover false prophets by observing the fruit of their teaching in lives—theirs and those of their disciples). Then, to cap off the whole sermon, Jesus insists on *doing* what He has said, not merely hearing it. But to know how is not the same as to show how. Jesus recognized this, and throughout the sermon insisted on *showing* how.

Now, in conclusion, let's draw together a few principles that will help us to understand *how to* use *how-to*.

1. Jesus gave specific instances of what He taught; He used case studies. He didn't merely state principles, abstractly as so many do today. You can actually picture (in your mind's eye) the man laying down his gift on the altar, getting up, leaving, looking for his brother, etc.

2. Jesus illustrated principles so they would be clear and memorable. Once having heard it, who could ever forget the splinter and the board of Matthew 7, or the principle it illustrates?

3. When giving a specific case (plucking out the eye that adulterously looks on a woman in lust), Jesus generalized (to the hand, and elsewhere to the foot) as well. He thereby extended the principle of making it difficult for one to sin again to all sorts of situations.

4. Jesus even gave actual models to follow (cf. the Lord's prayer).

Let us be thankful for the practicality of the Sermon on the Mount. Jesus showed us the importance of such practicality in Christian instruction. We too, in the ministry of the Word (in preaching and in counseling), must do the same.

It should be clear, then, that in His exposition of the Old Testament law Jesus, as the *kainos* man, creatively showed us how to understand, explain, apply, and implement the Scriptures in reference to everyday *kainos* living.

As I pointed out in that article, Christ often used brief case studies or examples. These came from real life and helped to make principles come to life as well as provided models for one to use in implementation. Moreover, at times, He even set forth step-by-step procedures for fulfilling God's will (cf. Matt. 5:23, 24). These are the things that counselors also must do.

Consider this case: Bill is concerned about his son Tommy. "He's the kind of kid that will let a bully in the neighborhood or at school beat him up. What do I do?" he asks. "Some say that I should teach him to fight back. But that doesn't seem right; it just doesn't fit the biblical picture. Do I just tell him to turn the other cheek and let them knock him over from that side too?"

In responding, the counselor wants to teach a biblical principle, but he also wants to be sure (1) that it is clear, so he uses an example, (2) that Bill implements the principle, and (3) that he does so properly. He begins with the example (or illustration): "Bill, suppose Tommy was having problems down at the local candy store, where the clerk behind the counter made it a practice to cheat him out of change. This comes to your attention. What would you tell him to do—to grab the extra money to which he is entitled out of the cash register the next chance he gets or to go on taking the loss?"

"Well, I don't think that I'd do either. After all, he's not quite seven, and he isn't ready to handle a situation like that."

"Let's suppose that it's the only place where he can buy candy for miles; it is convenient and he can walk to it. He doesn't want to stop buying candy, and there really isn't any reason for him to stop simply because of a dishonest clerk. You'll have to do something. What will you do?"

"I'll tell you what I'd do. I'd pay that clerk a visit, present the facts to him and tell him to straighten up and fly right or I will tell the manager about it."

"Ah, so you'd intervene personally, eh? Why?"

"Because, as I said, at his age he's not up to handling that sort of thing himself."

"Is he up to handling bullies?"

"Well. . . ."

"Of course he isn't. You shouldn't tell him to punch a bully back any more than you would tell him to dip into the cash register and take matters into his own hands. You yourself should get involved."

"I see; I never thought of that. I guess we've all been brainwashed by the macho idea."

"I agree. After all, what did God make parents for if not to protect their children? You protect him from the cold, from harmful germs, from tooth decay, etc., why shouldn't you protect him from bullies? You will protect him from the grocery store crook as well as all of these other dangers because they are all forces that are greater than he himself can handle. That's when you intervene."

Having made his point, the counselor is now concerned about implementing the principle of parental protection and, in addition, he wants to see it done properly. Therefore, he will speak to Bill about when to go, whom to see, what to say, etc. He will even role play the confrontations with the father of the neighborhood bully or the authorities at school if it seems necessary to be sure that Bill says the right things. And, in general, he will pursue every aspect of the situation about which Bill seems to need help. If Bill has a temper that has not been subdued biblically, he will focus on this point in discussing the confrontations that will be forthcoming. If that is not a problem and Bill is the sort of person who will run with the ball once he understands where the goal post is and what is expected of him on the play, he may not find it necessary to go beyond giving him the principle. Another way to put it is the more creatively *kainos* the counselee, the less creatively *kainos* the counselor needs to be.

Here, the new was an outgrowth of the old, and was best presented in the form of an example. This made the point in a way that Bill could grasp immediately and use as a model to generalize to this circumstance or to any similar situation. Moving from the known, the old (the clerk), to the unknown, the new (the bully), Bill was enabled to tie the two together by means of the example. The counselor's past is therefore important in creativity as well as in insight. The counselee's past is of vital importance too. Bill's counselor was reasonably sure of the response he would get from Bill about the candy store clerk, just as Nathan when he told the story of the "one little ewe lamb" to David (II Sam. 12:3ff.) and then drew the net with him swinging in it when he said, "You are the man!" The power of the old in helping to understand the new is of vital importance because of the continuity about which I have been speaking. Counselors, therefore, in creatively solving problems, will lean heavily on the past, both theirs and what they may reasonable presume to be the past of their counselees for ideas and for ways of explaining the new.

14

RENEWAL: THE CONDITION FOR CREATIVITY

In the preceding chapter I mentioned fulfillment and renewal and spent some time considering the former in relationship to counseling. In this chapter I should like to discuss *renewal*.

The basic two biblical words for renewal are compounds, having in their roots the same two terms, *neos* and *kainos,* to which I have introduced you already. The verbal forms are *anakainoo* (and a variant, *anakainizo*) and *ananeoo.* The noun that is encountered in the New Testament is *anakainosis.* These words occur in the following passages:

Anakainoo: II Corinthians 4:16; Colossians 3:10

Anakainizo: Hebrews 6:6

Ananeoo: Ephesians 4:23

Anakainosis: Romans 12:2; Titus 3:5

The first two verbs are built around *kainos,* ''to renew by making different''; in them a change in quality is in view. The third, stemming from *neos,* means to renew the youth of someone or something (and it can have the idea of renewal of a mortgage, or as in our day, a lapsed magazine subscription). The idea may be either the renewal of youthfulness or bringing something up-to-date. The renewal in Ephesians 4:23 is a renewal of the human spirit or attitude of mind.[1] (The word ''spirit'' often means ''attitude'' in such contexts.) The thought that Paul was conveying was not so much that the believer's mind is remade (though that is true enough) but that it is rejuvenated. It is given a youthful newness that is akin to the mind of Adam. In the fall, the desire to engage in mental activity of the sort that God built into Adam lapsed like one's unrenewed journal subscription. Now, in Christ, that spirit or attitude of thought is renewed. One can begin to think again as God intended him to

---

1. I no longer think that the word ''spirit'' here refers to the Holy Spirit, as I once did. The phrase ''spirit of your mind'' is too awkward. It is much easier to construe the words to mean ''attitude of your mind.'' Of course, either way, we recognize that the renewal of the believer's spirit is brought about by the Holy Spirit alone.

think, instead of leading a life governed by "meaningless ways of thinking" (Eph. 4:17).

Creative newness, then, comes from renewal in which true knowledge and holiness are "put on." Because these qualities, in themselves as old as Eden, are new to the regenerated sinner and to those around him, and because in the process of sanctification and Christian growth he is constantly presented with new ideas and patterns of living, the Christian —of all persons—regularly ought to be stimulated to creativity. If he will only open his eyes to what is happening as he studies the Bible, hears a sermon or learns the meaning of a new biblical truth, he will see that he is being confronted, indeed inundated, with *newness*. This process of renewal makes it easy for him to become a creative person, if he will only enter into it with enthusiasm. As a Christian, he is constantly required to face, examine, evaluate and accept or reject both old and new ways. Every faithful scribe (preacher) in the kingdom of heaven is regularly confronting him with things both old and new. This process of renewal provides the best possible atmosphere for developing creative skills. If creativity doesn't spring up, grow and mature under the changing conditions of *kainos* life, then under what conditions will it?

Clearly, during the process of renewal, the mind also is being made different by the purifying and ever-expanding understanding of God's truth. (Cf. Rom. 12:2, where *anakainosis* is used to describe a process of "making fresh, different.") This is the strength that the inner man needs every day to meet life's trials (*anakainoo* also appears in II Cor. 4:16). The fact that one is being renewed day by day means that daily God confronts His children with new concepts and new patterns of living. Therefore, if any one word rightly characterizes the *kainos* life, it is renewal, in both of its senses. The renewal of righteousness, knowledge and holiness mentioned in Colossians 3 and Ephesians 4 is, as those passages indicate, a renewal of the very aspects of the image and the likeness of God that Adam lost.

So, then, why aren't all Christians automatically creative? In view of the constant daily change taking place in their lives, creative change is what we would expect to see. But that isn't what we always find. Indeed, some of the dullest, most hidebound, rigid, uninteresting and uncreative (if not to say funereal) persons around are Christians. But, on the other hand, in the history of the world, many of the most creative also have been Christians. The facts seem to indicate that there has been a disproportionate number of highly creative persons who were Christians. This is true in literature, in the arts, in education, in science, in business and elsewhere, so that we must not overstate the case for non-creativity among Christians. Perhaps, if it seems at the present time that there is little creativity in the church, that is because it is harder to evaluate an age in which one himself is living.

It is true, nevertheless, that today there are many Christians who are not creative—and they will even tell you so themselves! How is that? Given the conditions mentioned above, one would expect creativity to ooze from every pore of every believer.

Creativity is not automatic. If it were, there would be no place for this book. Like the energy behind electricity, there has always been a power present, but it must be transformed into an available and useful form. It is in that transformational process that we are so deficient. The spiritual turbines needed for transforming the constant stream of confrontation for change pouring into a Christian's life into creative energy for Christ must be consciously acquired, put into place, maintained and kept in good repair. Though every Christian stands in the wind, most fail to erect windmills. Turbines and windmills do not grow up on their own like weeds in the woods. The wind of the Spirit is blowing; conditions are right for the fostering and maturing of creativity. But most lives are poorly equipped to harness the stream or the wind and convert it into spiritual energy. How does one transform God's daily flowing stream of grace into spiritual energy that may be used in creative ministry?

He begins by *recording* and *remembering*. That may sound strange, but wait before making a judgment. Even though one may have very little of a counseling "past," he does have *a personal past*. (Of course, as I have noted earlier, a counselor can acquire a past to some extent by borrowing from others.) God has done things for *him* and daily is doing more. God has used others to do things for Him and for others around him. If he will learn to open his heart, as well as his eyes and ears, to all of these things, he will see creativity—God's own, and the creativity of other Christians—all around him. Unlike Paul and David, and other great saints of God, uncreative Christians fail to observe and remember what God is doing (cf. II Cor. 4:16; Ps. 68:19[2]; Lam. 3:23). This is dangerous:

> Because they did not observe the Lord's doings,
> nor the work of His hands,
> He shall demolish them . . . (Ps. 28:5, Berkeley).

Many of the Psalms are the records of those who have noted and who delight to recall God's wondrous acts. And from time to time, the psalmists summon the rest of us to *"remember* His marvelous deeds which He has performed" (Ps. 105:5[a], Berkeley[3]). In times of trouble it is easier to do so (Ps. 143:5), but it is a mistake to limit remembering and recording to such occasions. Rather, with the psalmist, we should say,

> *Every day* will I bless You . . .
> I will *dwell*[4] on the glorious splendor
> of Your majesty,
> and on the *records* of Your wonders.
> . . . as for Your greatness,
> I will *recount* it (Ps. 145: 2, 5, 6).

But are we to open our eyes and our hearts only to observe and to give thanks, to record, recount and meditate on God's activities on behalf of His people—or is there something more? Yes, there is something more. We are to learn how to conduct our lives from the observation of God's ways in dealing with us. Listen to Paul:

> And fathers, don't provoke your children to anger, but rather bring them up with the Lord's discipline and counsel (Eph. 6:4).

The words, "the Lord's discipline" mean that we must observe how God disciplines and counsels His people, and then use the same biblical methods in discipling our children. And, remember the Lord's words in John 13:12-15:

> Then, when He had washed their feet and had put on His clothes and sat down at the table again, He said to them, "Do you understand what I have done to you? You call Me 'Teacher,' and 'Lord,' and you are right in doing so, because I am. But if I—your Teacher and

---

2. See the correct translation of this verse in a modern version.

3. Cf. esp. Ps. 111:4. God wants us to remember what He does.

4. The word "dwell" (Hebrew, *siach*) means to "muse, meditate, talk over with one's self." God's doings should become the subject of our daily consideration. Cf. my study of meditation in *Ready to Restore*.

Lord—washed your feet, you also ought to wash one another's feet.
I have set an example that you also should do as I have done to you.

Moreover, it is Christ's relationship to His church that forms the basic
pattern for the Christian husband's relationship to his wife. He is, for
instance, to be the same sort of head over his wife that Christ is over His
church. In order to know what that means, specifically, again, the
Christian counselor must study God's dealings with His church. Part of
that is the way Christ deals with him as a part of the church.

In all of this, it is necessary for one who wants to avail himself of the
creative energy that flows daily from Christ to *become aware* of it and
devote himself to a study of the same. This study, or as the psalmist put
it, "dwelling on it," alone will bring about the greater awareness of the
"variegated grace of God" (I Pet. 4:10) streaming forth from the right
hand of the throne of God, which is needed to appreciate the daily
"newness" of God's dealings with us (Lam. 3:23[5]). One who is fully
aware of this will know much about the newness that is essential to all
truly creative thought and action.

In this study (dwelling, or meditation), *recording* what one observes,[6]
and *recounting* it to others will help in *remembering* it. If a counselor
does so regularly, it will not be long before he will become aware of a
large variety of approaches that are applicable to the counseling room.
Quickly, he will build up a stockpile (or storehouse) of ideas and
practices that stem from God's own approaches. Such constant "dwelling" on God's activity in helping and in counseling His people will
develop a readiness for creative thought that, like God's manifold grace,
tends toward variety and newness in its solutions. The variety that God
exhibits in His dealing with men is not an indication of any instability or
undependableness on His part. Rather, it is a demonstration of His
greatness and the many-sided nature of His being, as well as evidence of
His concern for adapting His solutions to the varied circumstances in

---

5. The word, *chadash*, used here, means "fresh, unheard of." Cf. its use in the
Hebrew text of Isa. 66:22; *kainos* is almost exclusively used in the LXX to translate this
frequently occurring term. The only exception is found in Isa. 65:15.

6. Results of studies actually recorded can be most helpful. Make it a practice every
day to record at least one new idea. Sooner than one may think, ideas will come faster and
faster and will get better and better.

which men find themselves. According to Hebrews 1:1, 2, even in giving His revelation, God adopted a variety of modes. We, therefore, must learn from God Himself that, in doing His work, we must emulate His ways. That means we must study creative variety in His works.

So, on two counts, (1) the change and newness of life to which the Christian counselor is called (Ps. 6:4^c), and (2) the daily, variegated grace of God, the Christian, by virtue of this *kainos* life itself, is in the perfect place to develop a creative attitude and approach toward life.

The reason why Christians are dull and uncreative, therefore, is not that the *kainos* life is that way; indeed, exactly the opposite is true—it is *kainos*. Nor is it because the Christian is frozen in a tight, narrow position by adopting biblical standards. Again, the opposite is the case. Within a scriptural framework, it is clear to all unprejudiced persons who investigate it properly that God's commandments are "exceedingly broad" (Ps. 119:96).[7] God's Word opens new vistas and gives one a great amount of elbow room; it does not cramp him.[8] Well, then, let us ask again, Why is it that Christians are so uncreative?

Let me suggest three reasons:

1. Many Christians have seen no need for creativity. I have already mentioned several reasons for this. Let me now add one more to those. As in preaching, many Bible-believing people think that the *manner* in which truth is presented is irrelevant, so long as it is God's truth. Of course, God may do as He pleases, regardless of how we present His truth, and He often does work wondrously *in spite of* our ineffectiveness and inefficiency. But that does not excuse us. We ought to avoid becoming stumbling blocks to others by the poor ways in which we present God's truth to them. A study of Paul's concern over this matter in I Corinthians 2:2, 4, 5, and in Colossians 4:5, 6[9] will soon convince honest doubters of the importance of this matter. God's vibrant truth must not be sluggishly presented in abstract and impractical ways that distort and misrepresent it because, unlike our Lord,[10] we do not know

---

7. The Hebrew word for broad means "wide, spacious, extensive."

8. The term translated "exceedingly" also means "strong." The idea is that whatever it modifies is strongly so.

9. Cf. extensive comments on this subject as it is explained by Paul in Col. 4:5, 6 in my book, *Ready to Restore*. In this book, I have given an exposition of that passage.

10. Cf. previous remarks in this book on the Sermon on the Mount.

(or better, we have not taken the time or made the effort to learn) how to apply and implement it concretely.

The first reason I have in view, then, is that many Christians seem to care little about form and stress only content, failing to recognize with Paul that form molds content. Because of this they see no need to work on creativity. Their attitude toward the counselee may be expressed in these words: "Well, if God says do it, why doesn't he do it?" Of course, every counselee ought to do what God says, but what such persons forget (or have never taken the time to observe) is that many counselees who truly want to do what God commands do not know *how* to apply biblical principles to their own situation or even how to begin doing so. One man thinks, "I know I should tell my wife that I cheated on her and seek her forgiveness, but I'm afraid of the consequences, especially since I am so inept at communication. No, I'd better not; I'll probably do more harm than good." While words like these can be an excuse, we must not dismiss them in all cases as such. In more than enough instances, the statement is an accurate account of the facts. The man simply *is* inept, and knows it. The counselor must help him in matters of form in such cases. It is therefore important for every counselor to become concerned about *both* form and content.

2. Many Christians are not living the Christian life the way they should. Therefore, they do not experience the daily blessings of God as they might because, in effect, they are fighting against them and are nurturing sinful practices, which they do not want to abandon. The reason they do these things is that they are afraid of change. This fear can be aroused, as I have already noted, because they are lazy or because they are afraid of the unknown. Here I wish only to note that one's failure to appreciate the daily flow of God's grace will impair his ability to appropriate those elements in the milieu from which creativity springs forth.

3. But there are many others whose principal problem is that they don't know how to observe. They simply do not see or hear; it is as if they were blind and deaf to God at work in their daily lives. They are like deaf men at a symphony, like blind men at a flower show. But they are not really blind or deaf if they really know Christ; their problem is ineptness of perception. Their perceptual faculties are intact; they simply have

never learned how to use them to perceive spiritual activity. Exhorting them to open their eyes and unstop their ears will not do. What they need is not exhortation but hope, encouragement—and *direction;* especially direction. For all such I suggest the following regimen.

(1) Acquire a looseleaf notebook and a package of 3x5 file cards.

(2) Carry a supply of cards with you at all times.

(3) Each day, ask God to help you to "see" and to "hear" Him at work, to "see" and to "hear" the ways in which fellow believers solve problems God's way, and to "see" and to "hear" the ways in which He enables you to do so.

(4) Whenever you "see" or "hear" something, no matter how minute it may seem, make a note of it on a card. Be sure that you record at least one note every day.

(5) Toward the end of each day, copy all of your notes in better, well-thought-through wording, into your looseleaf notebook, using a separate page for each entry and giving a title to each page.

(6) Continue to do the above Monday through Friday.

(7) On Saturday, prayerfully take out your notebook. Spend an hour or so studying the five or more entries that you have made during the previous five days. Further revise wording, jotting down comments that occur to you as you do so (writing forces you to think more creatively), and study each matter in the light of the Scriptures, noting in detail what God says about it. Experience must always be subjected to scriptural evaluation.

(8) Be sure that every creative idea or practice that is biblically legitimate is entered on the page; reject all ideas that do not prove to be thoroughly biblical upon examination.

(9) On Sunday, note ideas from Sunday school, from sermons, which others suggest, and on the following Saturday do the same with them.

(10) As you begin to accumulate creative ideas and practices, arrange them alphabetically in your notebook according to topics for quicker retrieval.

(11) Refer to your notebook when you need to be stimulated to think, when you can use these ideas to meet a concrete counsel-

ing problem, and, occasionally, when you just need to be stirred afresh to God's goodness.

(12) Continue this practice for six months. At the end of this time ask

A. Do I want to continue this practice any longer?

B. How much good, creative material do I now have that I would not have if I had not faithfully pursued this practice?

C. Have I now learned better how to walk through life with my eyes and ears open (and mind thinking)?

I can assure you that anyone who faithfully does as I have suggested for six weeks will want to go on for six months. And anyone who does it for six months will be a far more creative person than he/she was before. Aim at the six weeks period as a trial. But *do not give up before the six weeks have elapsed* (it takes about 40 days to make a transition and to acquire a new skill); otherwise, you will not have given the experiment a fair trial. Nor should you follow the program sporadically; *do it every day, without fail, for six weeks*.

Not only will creativity begin to bud (or even blossom) during this time period, but your own spiritual life may begin to bloom as well, as with the psalmist you will be able to bless God every day because you will have "dwelt" on His greatness and the wonders of His ways, and experienced—*renewal*.

15

VARIETY AND ADAPTATION

I have spoken of insight as the ability to spot those factors upon which a counseling case turns by depending on a backlog of biblical and biblically derived information, accumulated through the study and use of the Scriptures in counseling. This storehouse of information, the counselor's "past," enables the scribe in the kingdom of heaven to identify and eliminate those unique elements in the situation that are not essential to the case, and to discover which factors are essential to the existence of the situation itself.

Creativity, on the other hand, is the ability to adapt the usual biblical principles and practices to the extraordinary individual features under which the usual appears in any specific case. In doing so, something new will emerge. If the problem is lying, the positive part of the biblical solution (the put on) is a matter of truth telling. Insight consists of discovering the fundamental problem(s). But creativity is different; it handles problems of adaptation. Both are problem-solving skills, but their focus and their concerns differ.

In one case, Tom has been lying to his wife about his salary (there have been increases that he has failed to report and others that he denied receiving), while Mary has been lying to him about how she spends the money he gives her (she has been putting money into a separate bank account for a rainy day). During the course of counseling, the truth comes to the surface, both confess their lies and deception and seek forgiveness of God and one another. Both are now anxious to apply the positive side of Ephesians 4:25 to their future relationship. But, specifically, in their case, what does learning to tell the truth mean? To Tom? To Mary? Here is where the matter must not be left vague by the counselor; if it is, he will set them up for further possible trouble. But, to answer these questions concretely means that there must be creative thought, planning, and commitment to a program.

For Tom, it will mean telling about raises in the future, of course, and for Mary it will be giving accurate accounts of household needs, along with her actual use of funds to meet these needs. But those statements are just that—statements, abstractions. The fact of the matter is that in fulfilling these goals, structuring against future failure, and the use of radical amputation (I have commented on this elsewhere already) something more than abstract statements about noble goals will be required.

What am I talking about? Well, for instance, if Mary is undisciplined and sloppy about keeping records, she will have to learn something about discipline and something about basic financial accounting. That, in itself, will take some time and effort in giving instruction and in monitoring progress. All of that will have to be worked out in detail. Just exactly what is needed will have to be worked out on the basis of the particulars that are uncovered. Such matters as Mary's individual strengths and weaknesses, her attitudes, her knowledge, etc., will have to be considered. Creativity, in part, then, is a matter of making accurate judgments about individuals and the particular situations in which they happen to find themselves. It is also a matter of adapting solutions in the right way to these persons and circumstances—not too much or too little, nor too soon or too late.

This accuracy in the ministry of truth comes about only though prayerful experience in ministry. It flows from thoughtful, careful decision-making based on factual data that have been mined at hard labor in data-gathering, and through feedback in discussion of the implementation of principles.

That last point, illustrated, might sound something like this: ". . . so you see, Mary, you'll need a large enough notebook with several columns that you can use to. . . ."

"We have books like that at home. I'll give her one. As a matter of fact, pastor, I'll be glad to teach Mary how to set up the books, if she wants me to."

"What do you think of Tom's offer, Mary?"

"Great. I've always wanted him to show me how to do it, but I was afraid to ask him."

"Fine, if you really think that you can do it Tom, that will save us some time. Now, then, instead of discussing bookkeeping, I'll move to the next point. Mary, you are going to have to learn to enter records *every* day. If you get behind you'll miss items and you will defeat the whole project and become discouraged. Do you have any idea about how this problem can be solved?''

"No."

"I don't either, pastor."

"If you attach an activity to something that you already do every day (like eating, combing your hair, etc.) and not allow yourself to do that task until you have done your record-keeping chore, you'll find it a lot easier to develop the habit. Now, do you have any idea what that could be?''

And so it goes. First, the pastor was prepared to give elementary instruction in bookkeeping (often it is best to assign this sort of task to a dedicated layman in the church), but he discovered that Tom could do it and that Mary was anxious to have him do so. That was a plus for better communication that he did not want to miss. In adopting his solution, he readjusted to feedback, moving on when he found the bookkeeping matter was in hand.

Now, of course, he had many options. Note that I broke off the story before mentioning the creative adaptation that was adopted. In the space below, write out three creative possibilities:

Mary's bookkeeping chore could be attached to:

1. _____

2. _____

3. _____

A study of Paul's proclamation of the gospel in the Book of Acts demonstrates that while Paul never modified the message (everywhere he preached Christ's sacrificial, substitutionary, penal death and His bodily resurrection), at the same time he never presented it in the same way twice.[1] Paul approached Jews one way, Gentiles another. And he spoke to one group of Jews (or Gentiles) differently than to the next. Moreover, Hebrew parallelism, the basic form of Hebrew poetry, pro-

---

1. The results of this study are available in my book, *Audience Adaptation in the Sermons and Speeches of Paul*.

vides a perfect illustration of the fact that any truth may be taught in more than one way.[2]

So, it should be plain that in counseling, insight and creativity work side-by-side in harmony when they function properly. But creativity demands adjustment and readjustment, and final implementation of solutions may take any number of biblically legitimate forms.

Variety and adaptation of truth is an important matter. Apart from such flexibility within biblical norms one could plug in a set number of scenarios like computer chips to meet all situations. That would be convenient, easier to teach and easier to learn, but it just so happens that God did not make stereotyped people and circumstances that could be handled in that way. Many prefabricated, mini-scenarios from the "past" may be used (lists, pads, etc.) singly or in combination, but each must be adapted to the particular persons and situations at hand. The total scenario will always contain unique elements.

A conference table (see *Competent* for details) may be useful in a number of cases, just as I have described it. In others, it would not work. In a larger number of situations, parts of it, or variations on the general theme, would be more helpful. Creativity is needed to spot the need for variation and to make the variation that fits. One of the greatest failings that I have noted in biblical counselors is insensitivity to this need for variety.

It is not variety for variety's sake that I am talking about, however. Variety must make biblical principles clearer and must enable counselees to put them into effect in their lives to meet the exigencies of a particular situation. Whenever, therefore, the use of a routine implementation "as is" is possible without loss of meaning or effect, use it. But, be sure it really does fit. Alterations are often necessary. Truth is distorted when it is not fit or appropriate.

---

2. The basic form of Hebrew parallelism used in Psalms and Proverbs presents the same truth in at least two different ways. Repetition and contrast are the genius of this fundamental form.

CONCLUSION

This short book has had as its major thrust the following purposes:

1. To demonstrate what insight and creativity are;

2. To show their place and importance in counseling;

3. To set forth a couple of ways (not necessarily the only ways, or perhaps, even the best ways) of learning how to gain insight and creativity.

Because I have no models for the work that I have done, there is no question that what I have accomplished, if anything, is preliminary and rough. But my hope is that it will help many to become aware of the needs and the possibilities that I have tried to point up, and that it will challenge others to improve on and advance these meager efforts. But, because there is no other work that attempts to teach biblical counselors the principles and practices of insight and creativity from a biblical perspective, at least for the moment, I suppose you are stuck with this book or nothing.

In conclusion, let me suggest that, in conjunction with the *Christian Counselor's Casebook,* the student can continue to work on his skills. If he will but apply the principles of this book to the cases he finds in the *Casebook,* trying to exercise and gain insight by locating the major, usual problems in each case, and if he will develop creative assignments for each person represented in each case, he will have gained quite a counseling "past" by the time he has worked his way through the 140 cases.

In spite of the many rough edges in this book, I sincerely believe that it is a contribution to the study of biblical counseling. It is my earnest hope that those who read and seriously follow the advice I have given will discover that as a result they have become better counselors.

APPENDIX

INSIGHT LIST

Learning well the lists and the observations that I have made in the early chapters of this book will give new counselors an "instant past." The material there will provide a good start. Prior to beginning a new counseling case, it would be well to review that material, so that this past may become operative. However, there are other problems that I have not mentioned, which you will routinely discover as you advance in counseling ability and in the number of cases you have concluded successfully. It is well for you to list these in the space provided below as you encounter them so that as your insight grows you may have them available in one place for future consultation.

Problem	Class most Prone to it	Biblical Solutions
1. Describe it:	Reasons why:	

2.	*Problem*	*Class most* *Prone to it*	*Biblical Solutions*

_____

3.

_____

4.

_____

5.   *Problem*

*Class most
Prone to it*   *Biblical Solutions*

_____

6.

_____

7.

_____

8.	*Problem*	*Class most* *Prone to it*	*Biblical Solutions*

_____

9.

_____

10.

_____

		Class most	
11.	*Problem*	*Prone to it*	*Biblical Solutions*

_____

12.

_____

13.

_____

14.	Problem	Class most Prone to it	Biblical Solutions

15.

16.

---

17.   *Problem*   *Class most*
                            Prone to it   *Biblical Solutions*

_____

18.

_____

19.

_____

20.

Problem	Class most Prone to it	Biblical Solutions

21.

22.